Anthropology

Polity's *Why It Matters* series

In these short and lively books, world-leading thinkers make the case for the importance of their subjects and aim to inspire a new generation of students.

Lynn Hunt, *History*
Tim Ingold, *Anthropology*
Neville Morley, *Classics*

Tim Ingold

——————

Anthropology

Why It Matters

polity

First published in 2018 by Polity Press

13

Polity Press
65 Bridge Street
Cambridge CB2 1UR, UK

Polity Press
101 Station Landing
Suite 300
Medford, MA 02155, USA

ISBN-13: 978-1-5095-1979-8
ISBN-13: 978-1-5095-1980-4 (pb)

A catalogue record for this book is available from the British Library.

Library of Congress Cataloging-in-Publication Data

Names: Ingold, Tim, 1948- author.
Title: Anthropology: why it matters / Tim Ingold.
Description: Medford : Polity Press, [2018] | Series: Why it matters |
   Includes bibliographical references and index.
Identifiers: LCCN 2017057447 (print) | LCCN 2018001870 (ebook) | ISBN
   9781509519835 (Epub) | ISBN 9781509519798 (hardback) | ISBN
9781509519804
   (pbk.)
Subjects: LCSH: Anthropology--Philosophy. | Ethnology.
Classification: LCC GN345 (ebook) | LCC GN345 .I3726 2018 (print) | DDC
   301.01--dc23
LC record available at https://lccn.loc.gov/2017057447

Typeset in 11 on 15 Sabon by Servis Filmsetting Ltd, Stockport, Cheshire
Printed and bound in the Great Britain by TJ Books Ltd, Padstow, Cornwall

For further information on Polity, visit our website: politybooks.com

Contents

1 On Taking Others Seriously   1
2 Similarity and Difference   26
3 A Discipline Divided   52
4 Rethinking the Social   79
5 Anthropology for the Future   106

Notes   132
Further Reading   137
Index   139

1

On Taking Others Seriously

How should we live? No doubt human beings have always pondered this question. Perhaps it is the very pondering that makes us human. For other animals, it seems, the question scarcely arises. Each is more or less absorbed in its own way of doing things. But human ways of life – ways of doing and saying, thinking and knowing – are not handed down on a plate; they are not pre-ordained, nor are they ever finally settled. Living is a matter of deciding how to live, and harbours at every moment the potential to branch in different directions, no one of which is any more normal or natural than any other. As paths are made by walking, so we have continually to improvise ways of life as we go along, breaking trails even as we follow the footsteps of predecessors. We do so, however, not in isolation but in the company of others. Like the strands of a rope,

1

lives intertwine and overlap. They go along together and mutually respond to one another in alternating cycles of tension and resolution. No strand carries on for ever; thus as some pass away, others join. That's why human life is social: it is the never-ending and collective process of figuring out how to live. Every way of life, then, represents a communal experiment in living. It is no more a solution to the problem of life than is the path a solution to the problem of how to reach a destination as yet unknown. But it is an *approach* to the problem.

Let us summon up a field of study that would take upon itself to learn from as wide a range of approaches as it can; one that would seek to bring to bear, on this problem of how to live, the wisdom and experience of all the world's inhabitants, whatever their backgrounds, livelihoods, circumstances and places of abode. This is the field I advocate in these pages. I shall call it *anthropology*. It may not be anthropology as you might have imagined it, or even as it is practised by many of those who profess to be anthropologists. Conceptions and misconceptions of the discipline abound, and it would be tedious to review them all. I make no apology for presenting a personal view, coloured by my own career as a student and teacher in the subject, perhaps less of what anthropology is than

2

of what I think it should aspire to be. Others may differ, but that would be a sign of vitality, not of weakness. For whatever else it may be, anthropology will always be a discipline-in-the-making: it can be no more finished than the social life with which it is concerned. Thus the history of anthropology cannot be told as a story from beginning to end. Nor can we rest on our laurels, as if to suppose that after centuries of error, ignorance and prejudice we have finally emerged into the light. There is work to be done, and this book is as much about remaking anthropology for the future as it is about retelling its past.

Now you might think that the problem of how to live really belongs to philosophy, and you would not be wrong. It is a problem, after all, that touches on the very foundations of human existence in this world of ours. We call ourselves human beings, but what does it mean to be human? The name science has given us, as a species, is *Homo sapiens*, but in what does our alleged sapience, or wisdom, consist? How do we know, think, imagine, perceive, act, remember, learn, converse in language and live with others in such distinctive and yet various ways? By what means, and on what principles, do we organize ourselves into societies, build institutions, administer justice, exercise power, commit

3

acts of violence, relate to the environment, worship the gods, care for the sick, confront mortality, and so forth? These questions are endless, and philosophers have addressed them at length. So too have anthropologists. But here's the difference. Philosophers are reclusive souls, more inclined to turn inwards into a studious interrogation of the canonical texts of thinkers like themselves – mostly, though not exclusively, dead white men – than to engage directly with the messy realities of ordinary life. Anthropologists, to the contrary, do their philosophizing in the world. They study – above all through a deep involvement in observation, conversation and participatory practice – with the people among whom they choose to work. The choice depends on particularities of experience and interest, but in principle, they could be any people, anywhere. Anthropology, in my definition, is *philosophy with the people in*.

Never in human history has this kind of philosophy been more needed. Evidence that the world is at a tipping point is all around us, and overwhelming. With an estimated human population of 7.6 billion – set to rise to more than 11 billion by the end of the century – there are more of us than ever before, living on average for longer than ever before. More than half of the world's population now resides in cities, most no longer drawing a livelihood directly from the land as their predecessors did. Supply chains for food and other produce criss-cross the globe. Forests are being laid waste, swathes of cultivable land have been turned over to soybean and palm-oil production, mining has gouged the earth. Human industry, above all the burning of fossil fuels on a massive scale, is affecting the world's climate, increasing the probability of potentially catastrophic events, and in many regions shortages of water and other necessities of life have sparked genocidal conflicts. The world remains in the grip of a system of production, distribution and consumption that, while grotesquely enriching a few, has not only left countless millions of people surplus to requirements, condemned to chronic insecurity, poverty and disease, but also wreaked environmental destruction on an unprecedented scale, rendering many regions uninhabitable and clogging lands and oceans with indestructible and hazardous waste. These human impacts are irreversible and will likely outlast the tenure of our species on this planet. Not without reason have some declared the onset of a new era in the earth's history: the Anthropocene.

This world-on-a-knife-edge is the only world we have. However much we might dream of life on other planets, there is none other to which we might escape. Nor is there any going back to the past, from which to try an alternative route to the present. We are where we are, and can only carry on from there. As Karl Marx observed long ago, human beings are the authors of their own history, but under conditions not of their own choosing.[1] We cannot opt to be born into another time. Our present conditions were shaped by the actions of past generations that cannot be undone, just as our own actions, in turn, will irrevocably shape the conditions of the future. How, then, should we live now, such that there can be life for generations to come? What could make life sustainable, not for some to the exclusion of others, but for everyone? To address questions of this magnitude, we need all the help we can get. It is not as though the answers are lying around somewhere, needing only to be discovered. We will not find the secret in any doctrine or philosophy, in any branch of science or indigenous worldview. Nor can there be any final solution. History is full of monumental attempts to put an end to it, attempts that must necessarily fail if life is to continue. To find our way around the ruins is a task for all of us. That's where anthropology comes in, and why – in our precarious world – it matters so much.

The problem is not that we are starved of information or knowledge. To the contrary, the world is awash with it, and with digital enhancement the wash has become a flood. According to a recent study, some 2.5 million scientific papers are published every year, and the number published since 1665 has passed the 50 million mark.[2] Experts, armed with specialized data acquisition devices and sophisticated modelling techniques, are keen to offer their projections. We should listen to them, as we should listen to scholars steeped in disciplines of the arts and humanities whose reflections provide the contexts that better enable us to frame our current predicament. Yet all, scientists and humanists alike, have something in common, namely a sense that they can take the measure of the world from some place beyond it, up above or far ahead, whence they can look back and pronounce upon its workings with an authority denied to those whose business is more intimately tied to the mundane affairs of everyday life. From their vantage point, they profess to be able to explain what for the rest of us lies beyond comprehension. Physicists explicate the workings of the universe, biochemists the workings of life, neuroscientists the brain, psychologists the mind, political scientists the state, economists the market, sociologists society, and so on. Anthropology, too, for much of its disciplinary history, has claimed similarly exalted powers, namely to spell out the contexts, variously labelled 'social' or 'cultural', within which the works and lives of other people could be interpreted or even accounted for.

In what follows I shall have more to say about this claim. It is not, however, one to which I subscribe. The kind of anthropology I propound here has a different purpose. This is not to interpret or explain the ways of others; not to put them in their place or consign them to the 'already understood'. It is rather to share in their presence, to learn from their experiments in living, and to bring this experience to bear on our own imaginings of what human life could be like, its future conditions and possibilities. Anthropology, for me, thrives on this engagement of imagination and experience. What it brings to the table is not a quantum of knowledge, to be added to the contributions of other disciplines, all bent on dredging the world for information to be turned into knowledge products. My kind of anthropology, indeed, is not in the business of 'knowledge production' at all. It aspires to an altogether different relation with the world. For anthropologists as for the people among whom they work, the world is not the object of study but its milieu. They are, from the start, immersed in its processes and relations. Critics may see this as a weakness, or a vulnerability. For them, it reveals a lack of objectivity. But for us, this is the very source from which anthropology takes its strength. For objective knowledge is not what we are after. What we seek, and hope to gain, is wisdom. These are by no means the same; they may even operate at cross-purposes.

Knowledge seeks to fix things within the concepts and categories of thought, to hold them to account, and to make them to some degree predictable. We often speak of arming ourselves with knowledge, or of using it to shore up our defences so that we can better cope with adversity. It gives us power, control, and immunity to attack. But the more we take refuge in the citadels of knowledge, the less attention we pay to what is going on around us. Why bother to attend, we say, when we already know? To be wise, to the contrary, is to venture out into the world and take the risk of exposure to what is going on there. It is to let others into our presence, to pay attention and to care. Knowledge fixes and puts our minds at rest; wisdom unfixes and unsettles. Knowledge arms and controls; wisdom disarms and surrenders. Knowledge has its challenges, wisdom has its ways, but where the challenges of knowledge close in on their solutions, the ways of wisdom open up to a process of life. Now I am not of course suggesting that we can do without knowledge. But we need wisdom as well. At the present juncture, the balance has tipped precipitously towards the former, and away from the latter. At no previous time in history, indeed, has so much knowledge been married to so little wisdom. It is the task of anthropology, I believe, to restore the balance, to temper the knowledge bequeathed by science with the wisdom of experience and imagination.

Among scholars of different stripes, anthropologists are distinguished by their readiness to learn from those who, in a world fixated on the advance of knowledge, might otherwise be dismissed as uneducated, illiterate or even ignorant. These are people whose voices, unused to dominant media of communication, would otherwise remain unheard. As anthropologists have demonstrated time and again, such people are wise beyond their allegedly more knowledgeable superiors. And with the world on a cusp, theirs is wisdom we can ill afford to ignore. We have much to learn, if only we allow ourselves to be educated by others with experience to share. Yet these others have been shunned by scholars who, for the most part, have been content to enlist them in their researches more as informants than as teachers, interrogated for what can be elicited from their minds rather than sought out for what they can show us of the world. Elaborate methods have been devised to keep them at arm's length. Methods are the guarantors of objectivity, put in place to ensure that research results should not be contaminated by too close or affective an involvement of researchers with those they study. For anthropology, however, such involvement is of the essence. All study calls for observation, but in anthropology we observe not by objectifying others but by paying attention to them, watching what they do and listening to what they say. We study *with* people, rather than making studies *of* them. We call this way of working 'participant observation'. It is a cornerstone of the discipline.

Participant observation takes time. It is not uncommon for anthropologists to spend many years in what they call the 'field'. Initially set down in an unfamiliar place as a possibly uninvited guest, the fieldworker is largely beholden to his or her hosts. Anthropologists have written at length on the institution of the gift, and have shown how the principles of giving and receiving are at the core of everyday life. But these principles are equally fundamental to the practice of anthropological fieldwork. It is a practice founded on generosity, on receiving with good grace what is given rather than seeking to obtain, by deceit or subterfuge, what is not. This is what distinguishes the field from the laboratory. In the field you have to wait for things to happen,

11

and accept what is offered when it is offered. That's why fieldwork takes so long. The laboratory, by contrast, is a place artfully set up, equipped with an experimental apparatus by means of which things are either forced or tricked into revealing their secrets, otherwise known to science as 'data'. Though, literally, a datum is a thing given (from the Latin *dare*, 'to give'), in the vocabulary of science it has come to mean that which is there for the taking – a 'fact' that has already precipitated out from the ebb and flow of life in which it once was formed. Only when things have thus hardened into discrete facts can they be counted. For this reason we tend to think of data, in the first place, as quantitative.

Should we regard participant observation, then, since it is practised in the field rather than the laboratory, as a method for collecting data that are not quantitative but qualitative: data that cannot be tabulated in numbers, expressed as measurements, or compiled into statistics? This is how textbooks of anthropology usually describe it. Yet something makes me uneasy about the very idea of 'qualitative data'. For the quality of a phenomenon can only lie in its *presence* – in the way it opens up to its surroundings, including we who perceive it. The moment we turn the quality into a datum, however, the phenomenon is closed off, severed from the

12

matrix of its formation. Collecting qualitative data is like opening up to people only to turn your back on them, attending to what they say *for what it says about them*. Generosity becomes a front for expropriation. Few would go to the lengths of Irenäus Eibl-Eibesfeldt, the Austrian founder of 'human ethology', who was so intent on gathering data on people behind their backs that he designed a camera with a 90-degree reflector, allowing him to photograph his subjects unawares while pointing to someone or something else. This was a monstrous deception. But there remains a certain duplicity in pretending to join the conversation with one's hosts, in good faith, while actually using it as a means to gather intelligence on them. Anthropologists often stress the importance, in fieldwork, of establishing rapport. But rapport can mean both friendship and report. Is it right to befriend people in order to write them up?

The word that anthropologists use for writing people up is *ethnography*. Is participant observation, then, a means to the end of ethnography? Most anthropologists would say so; indeed in many minds method and result are so confused that the very practice of participant observation amounts to ethnographic work. But I disagree. To repeat, participant observation is a way of studying *with* people. It is not about writing other lives, but about joining with them in the common task of finding ways to live. Herein, I contend, lies the difference between ethnography and anthropology. Thus for the anthropologist, participant observation is absolutely *not* a method of data collection. It is rather a commitment to learning by doing, comparable to that of the apprentice or student. After all, we don't go to study with our professors at the university with a view to rendering an account of what they say, or to writing them up for posterity. We rather allow ourselves to be *educated* by them. For us as for our teachers, that education is transformative. The same is surely true of the education to which we submit through participant observation in the field. In short, the overriding purpose of anthropology is not ethnographic but educational. Anthropology matters, in my view, precisely because of its potential to educate, and through this education, to transform lives – our own and those of the people among whom we work. But this potential will only be realized if we are willing to learn from them. And we will learn nothing unless we take them seriously.

Taking others seriously is the first rule of my kind of anthropology. This doesn't just mean attending to their deeds and words. More than that, we have to face up to the challenges they present to our assumptions about the ways things are, the kind of world we inhabit, and how we relate to it. We do not have to agree with our teachers, or assume they're right and we're wrong. We are entitled to differ. But we cannot duck the challenge. Admittedly, the inglorious history of anthropology offers and exemplifies plenty of stratagems for doing just that. They include the pretence that the people are less than rational or incapable of logical thought, that they are in the grip of ancient superstition, that their thinking is characteristic of earlier stages in human development from childlike innocence to maturity, that they are operating on the basis of false or defective information, that their behaviour is programmed by tradition, that they are unable to tell fact from fantasy or to draw a line between the literal and the metaphorical. Most contemporary anthropologists rightly disown these stratagems, insisting on principle that other people cannot be ranked on any scale of reason, intelligence or maturity that might justify taking their thought and practice less seriously than our own. Nevertheless, many still subscribe to what could be called the 'willing suspension of disbelief', analogous to that of theatre-goers who, for the duration of the per- formance, allow themselves to be swept up into the

15

make-believe world enacted on stage as if it were real life.

To take this stance, however, is to deny that the words and deeds of others, especially when they grate with our understanding, have any hold on reality. It, too, is a stratagem for protecting our backs, for convincing ourselves that regardless of what people say or do, reality-as-we-know-it remains inviolate. Donning the mantle of omniscience, we declare that the world perceived and enacted by the people, and which for them is entirely real, is in truth a construction built of concepts, beliefs and values that add up to what is commonly called their 'culture'. Human worlds, we insist, are culturally constructed – except, of course, our own, since, bathed in the light of reason, we can see what they cannot, namely that these diverse constructions are but alternative fabrications of a given reality. Their view is suspended in a web of meaning, ours is grounded in objective fact. We are spectators in the gallery of human variation; they are the portraits. We can see in, they can't see out. This stratagem is reproduced every time we treat the things people do and say not as lessons from which we can learn but as *evidence from which to build a case*. It amounts to treating these things as symptoms of something else, of the hidden hand of culture that, unbeknownst to the people themselves, is driving their thought and practice. This, indeed, is to betray the first rule of anthropology. For to take others seriously means not to close the case but to open up to imaginings enriched by their experience.

The questions at stake, here, go beyond those of how we can *know* the world. More fundamentally, they are questions of how there can *be* a world for us to know. In the inscrutable vocabulary of philosophy, questions of the first kind, of knowing, are *epistemological*; those of the second, of being, are *ontological*. While the shift from epistemology to ontology might sound arcane, it is of profound importance. Let me give an example to show why. During the 1930s, one of the most prescient anthropologists of the twentieth century, A. Irving Hallowell, was working among the Anishinaabe or Ojibwa people, indigenous hunters and trappers of north-central Canada. There he developed a close friendship with William Berens, Chief of the Berens River Anishinaabe (see Figure 1). Berens was a man of great wisdom and intellect, taught by his own elders and by a lifetime of attention to the world around him, including its animals, its plants, and particularly its stones. By Hallowell's account, his discussions with Berens profoundly influenced his own thinking. One such discussion found the pair

Figure 1 Chief William Berens seated beside the living stones of his elders; a picture taken by A. Irving Hallowell in 1930, between Grand Rapids and Pikangikum, Ontario, Canada. (American Philosophical Society)

returning to the subject of stones, prompted by the observation that in the grammar of the Ojibwa language, as formalized by linguists, the word for 'stone' appeared to be of a class normally applied to animate rather than inanimate entities. Puzzled by this, Hallowell asked, 'Are all the stones we see about us here alive?' After long reflection, Berens answered thus: 'No! But some are.'[3] The answer, Hallowell recalls, left a lasting impression. But he was not sure what to make of it.

How could anyone seriously suggest that something as inert as a stone could possibly be alive? And if some can be alive, why should not this be so of all? One way of dealing with these questions might be to suppose that the attitudes people take towards things may be of two kinds. There is a common-sense practical attitude, typical of everyday life, and an attitude charged by faith and ideology, reserved for occasions of a ritual or ceremonial nature imbued with symbolic associations. In a treatise on the rudiments of religion first published in 1912, Émile Durkheim – founder in France of the discipline of sociology – called these attitudes, respectively, profane and sacred.[4] Take tables, for example. We usually think of tables as inanimate objects, but if the table happens to be an altar, within the setting of a religious ceremony, we might well attribute to it extraordinary powers, as if it radiated spiritual vitality. Could it be the same with the Ojibwa and their stones? It must be as obvious to the Ojibwa as to people everywhere that stones, as ordinarily encountered in the natural environment, are inanimate. Yet some stones, on some occasions, might be sanctified, and appear to those who treat them so to be invested with a sort of aura or life-force. Is that what Berens meant when he pronounced that some stones are alive? Could his statement be taken as evidence of a ritual attitude, which leads people collectively to deceive themselves into taking for reality what they know from ordinary life to be fantastical?

In our secular age it is all too easy to write off what others say and do, when it contravenes our sensibilities, as mere ritual. Our portraits of exotic cultures tend to be daubed in ritual colours. But as Hallowell knew, it would have been an insult to his friend's intelligence to follow this route. For his was not a statement of doctrine. He did not assert that stones are alive, period, as if this were a foregone conclusion, mandated by tradition, and in the face of all countervailing evidence. On the contrary, Berens reached his judgement only after long deliberation. And as he was at pains to explain to Hallowell, it was a judgement founded upon personal experience. He had observed that some stones could move of their own accord, and even produce sounds akin to speech. We, of course, who are convinced that stones cannot do such things, might suppose that he just imagined it, or dreamt it up. But were Berens with us now, he would doubtless want to know how, in our philosophy, experience and imagination can so readily be distinguished. Do we not experience our dreams? Is the world of our dreams really so different from that of our waking life? For those of us raised in societies in which scientific authority is paramount, the road to truth lies in separating fact from fantasy. But could it not be otherwise? What if truth lies in the unison of experience and imagination, in a world to which we are alive and that is alive to us?

This is not an objective truth, to be sure. But it is one of which we can be fully part, rather than one from which, as thinking subjects, we are inclined to exclude ourselves. As such, it can only be provisional. We can never speak with certainty of the world, as if we knew already, not because our hypotheses about it might later turn out to be false or our predictions awry, as scientists would say, but because the world itself is never settled in its structure and composition. It is, rather, continually coming into being – as indeed are we ourselves, being part of it. For precisely that reason, this ever-forming world is a perpetual source of wonder and astonishment. We should attend to it. This is what Berens teaches us, if only we are prepared to treat his words with the gravity they deserve. They lead us to question much that we otherwise take for granted. What is it about our own approach to reality that makes the idea of moving, speaking stones so obviously fantastical? After all, stones do wander, descending scree-strewn slopes under their own weight, or carried by water, ice or ocean waves. And they do make sounds when struck, against each other or by other things. It is as though each stone had a distinctive voice, as humans do. If by speech we mean the way we humans have of making our presence audibly felt, then might not the same be said of stones in their resounding? In this sense, they too could speak.

To pay attention to things – to watch for their movements and listen to their sounds – is to catch the world in the act, like riding the cusp of a wave ever on the point of breaking. Far from coming late upon a world wherein the die is already cast, it is to be there, present and alert, at the very moment of its taking shape. In that moment experience and imagination fuse, and the world comes to life. By harnessing our perception to the currents of world-formation we, like Berens, can witness the liveliness of things, including stones and much else besides. But this means thinking of life in a way very different from that imagined by science. It is not some secret ingredient, hidden within things deemed to be in possession of it, whence they are mobilized on the world's stage. It is to think of life, rather, as the potential of the circulations of materials and currents of energy that course through the world to bring forms into being and hold them in place for their allotted span. It is not, then, that life is in stones. Rather, stones are in life. In anthropology, this understanding of the being and becoming of things – this ontology, if you will – is known as *animism*. Once dismissed as the most primitive of religions, founded on a mistaken belief in the spirituality of objects, animism is now regarded as a poetics of life that betters even science in its comprehension of the fullness of existence. That's what comes from taking others seriously.

Two grown men – an American professor and an Ojibwa elder – conversing about stones? The example might seem trivial, even absurd. But I hope to have convinced you that their conversation opens up to fundamental questions about the world we live in, about our own place in it, indeed about life itself. It is of course just one example of countless conversations that anthropologists have had with people the world over, every one of which could potentially yield to questions of equal magnitude. The shift to questions of being that began with Hallowell has since gathered such momentum that many anthropologists today are speaking of a 'turn to ontology'. For Hallowell himself – despite his prescience a man of his time – this was a turn too far. In the end, and tragically, he turned his back on his friend. The title of his paper – 'Ojibwa ontology, behavior, and worldview' – says it all. In it, Chief Berens reappears as an anonymous 'old man' whose attitude towards stones merely attests to the received view of his culture. We can no longer afford to be so complacent today. For it has become evident, as never before, that the existential certainties upon which the modern era was founded have taken the world to the brink. We need to forge alternative approaches to the problem of how to live, which might heal the rupture between ways of knowing the world and ways of being in it, between science and nature. This healing is a necessary step along a path towards a future that is open-ended and sustainable.

To be clear: I am not suggesting that so-called 'indigenous' people such as the Ojibwa, whose ancestors had been living from the land for millennia prior to the arrival of European colonizers, have all the right answers to the questions of how to live. Nor am I suggesting that so-called 'westerners', whose ancestors were complicit in the colonial enterprise, have got them all wrong. No-one has the answers. But we do have our different approaches, based on personal experience and what we have learned from others, and these are worth comparing. Anthropology as a discipline is driven by a commitment to the worth of this comparative exercise. To compare, however, is not to juxtapose settled forms of thought and practice, as if they were already sedimented into the minds and bodies of people of this or that tradition. For thinking is no more confined to the replication of the already thought than is practice to the already done. What we compare, rather, are *ways* of thinking and doing that continually overtake any ends thrown in their paths. This is not to catalogue the diversity of human lifeways but to join the conversation. It is a conversation, moreover, in which all who join stand to be transformed. The aim of anthropology, in short, is to make a conversation of human life itself. This conversation – this life – is not just *about* the world. In a sense that I shall go on to elaborate in the chapters to follow, it *is* the world. It is the one world we all inhabit.

2

Similarity and Difference

Everyone is different. But are some more different than others? Can we say that these people here have more in common with one another than any of them do with those people there? This, after all, is how we have always been taught to sort people into cultures. The members of a culture, we are inclined to say, have a lot in common: usually they speak the same language, they may profess to the same lifestyle, follow the same religious observances, adhere to the same values, and so on. It might even be said that thanks to these commonalities, they inhabit their own cultural world, just one of a multitude of such worlds which, taken together, make up the mosaic of humanity. Anthropologists have long been at the forefront in making the case for cultural diversity. Indeed they sometimes seem constitutionally averse to singularity: never one world, they insist; always many worlds. I believe this appeal to plurality, however, to be misguided. It is not only wrong in principle; it is also perilous for the discipline, leaving us powerless to oppose the hegemony of global forces that have delivered mass inequality, disenfranchisement and indebtedness. An anthropology worthy of the name must, in my view, be founded on the principle that we inhabit one world. But this world is not the globe of corporate finance, of international telecommunications, of 'the West'. It is a world not of similarity but of manifold difference. For anthropology, the challenge is to spell out, with clarity and conviction, the one-ness of such a world.

To begin to address the challenge, however, we need to think again about what it means to say of people that they are the same or different, and that will be my task in this chapter. For anthropologists, the task is inextricably bound to two keywords that have dogged the discipline from its inception. These are 'nature' and 'culture'. The meanings of both words are many and contentious, and I shall not even attempt to review them here. Suffice it to say that nature has long carried a sense of the essential qualities that things of a certain kind have in common – qualities, moreover, that are thought to be fixed from the outset, stable and unchanging.

What is natural to things is thus considered not only universal but also innate, and with the rise of the physical and biological sciences, this innate component has come increasingly to be seen to lie in their material constitution. Culture, on the other hand, has ever been a mark of distinction or particularity. With its roots in the idea of cultivation, as in the raising of crops, the particular qualities to which the word refers are supposed to have been not so much given from the start as developed or acquired. Where nature is fixed, culture is thus subject to growth, variation and historical change. And the more that the fixity of nature is attributed to material conditions, the more culture comes to be understood as overwriting the material, much as ideas on paper. Culture, it seems, is a pattern of the mind.

The dichotomy between culture and nature, in short, conflates two oppositions: of the particular to the universal, and of mind to matter. Many of the confusions and contradictions to which the discourses of nature and culture have given rise stem from the non-alignment of these oppositions. Ecologists and conservationists, for example, regard nature as a world of biodiversity; psychologists regard the mind as a domain of cognitive universals. Where for the former all organisms are different, for the latter all minds are alike. And anthropologists? They are caught in the same dilemma. There is a natural world, they admit, and human beings – like other animals – are part of it. Yet they also insist that it is of the essence of humanity to have transcended this world, to have broken the bonds of nature that hold all other creatures captive. The human being, it seems, is one thing; being human another. The first is an individual of a species, *Homo sapiens* – one of countless species making up the animal kingdom. But it is by the second, we say, that the human *exceeds* the animal. Is it in the nature of the human, then, to be a kind of animal or to achieve a condition that is more than animal? This very question reveals the predicament of a creature that can know itself, and the world of which it is part, only by taking leave of that world and viewing it, as it were, from the far side. The *Anthropos* from which anthropology takes its name is the epitome of this predicament.

According to philosopher Giorgio Agamben, our modern idea of humanity is the product of an 'anthropological machine' that relentlessly drives us apart, in our capacity for self-knowledge, from the world which we and other creatures inhabit.[1] We think of ourselves as human subjects, adrift in a world of material objects. This division has been both the source of the split between cultural and biological dimensions of human existence, and the obstacle which has so far derailed all attempts to achieve a more participatory understanding of human life in the world. To break the deadlock calls for nothing less than a dismantling of the machine. In this spirit I believe the task of anthropology is to *go beyond* the idea of humanity, or at least to frame it differently. The first step in doing so is to take nature and culture not as answers but as questions. The question of nature is: in what respects are humans similar? What leads them to do things in much the same ways? And the question of culture is: in what respects do humans vary? Why do they do things differently? We may observe, for example, that all human beings, after infancy and barring accident or disability, walk on two feet, but that only some peoples habitually carry loads on their heads. It is reasonable to ask why. But to conclude that everyone walks bipedally because it is human nature to do so, or that some peoples (but not others) carry loads on their heads because it is in their culture, would be manifestly circular.

The mistake is to suppose that nature and culture stand not for questions we ask about human beings but for causal agents actually lodged within human bodies and minds, whence they pull the strings of

30

behaviour, determining all we think and do. These agents have gone by various names. Human nature is often said to lie 'in our genes'. These genes have no direct connection with what molecular biologists call the genome – those strings of nucleotide bases (some three billion in humans) making up the DNA in the nucleus of every cell. Rather, they designate heritable attributes, commonly described as 'traits'. Taken together, these traits add up to a kind of design specification for a universal human being. Something analogous has been proposed for culture. The idea is that if the universal traits of human nature are carried by genes, then particular traits of culture must be specified by equivalent particles of information, lodged in the mind rather than the body, and passed on through imitative learning rather than genetic replication. It has recently become popular, following biologist Richard Dawkins, to call these particles 'memes'.[2] Regardless of whether traits are ascribed to genes or memes, however, we end up in the same circle. With both, what are observed and described as regularities of behaviour are pre-installed into bodies and minds as their underlying causes. Thus are accounts *of* human ways of thinking and doing turned, by sleight of hand, into explanations *for* them. Gene-and-meme theorists have discovered nothing less than that people do things because they do them!

Now there is no denying that most anthropologists have been driven by what has been called a 'passion for difference'.[3] They relish in showing how, for whatever we might assume is natural for humans to do, there are always people who do things otherwise. They are sceptical of attempts to 'naturalize' humanity, observing that most merely project things *we* take to be natural onto everyone else, casting as less-than-human any who do not adhere to them. It is no wonder, then, that anthropologists tend to be nervous about proposing true universals. In a bid to redress the balance, the American anthropologist Donald Brown – in a 1991 book entitled *Human Universals* – listed several hundred attributes for which, he claimed, there was no known exception.[4] It is a bizarre list, including not only such staples as 'language', 'symbolism' and 'toolmaking' but also 'hairstyles', 'Oedipus complex' and 'snakes, wariness around'. Not one of them, of course, is based on an exhaustive survey of all humans at all times, as such a task would clearly be impossible. For some, indeed, exceptions abound. An example is 'culture/nature distinction'. We know that many peoples including the Ojibwa, whom we met in the previous chapter, have no concepts corresponding to ours of nature and culture, and would repudiate any distinctions of the sort that, in the history of western ideas, have been affixed to them. But while it is always easy to find exceptions to any generalization, the deeper issue concerns the significance to be attached to the alleged universals. What are we to make of them?

Brown is primarily interested in those universals he calls innate, and he is convinced that they are programmed into a design for the human that evolved, by a Darwinian mechanism of variation under natural selection, over hundreds of thousands of years – in that geological era known as the Pleistocene – during which our ancestors lived above all by hunting wild animals and gathering wild plants. Life was precarious in those days, populations were thin on the ground and predatory animals a real threat. People needed their wits about them; they needed to be able to work together, and to augment their bodily powers – puny by comparison with the animals they hunted and that hunted them – with artificial instruments. It is easy to imagine the advantages for cooperation conferred by verbal communication, and for hunting of being able to design and make one's own tools. And it would have made obvious practical sense for barefoot hunters and gatherers to be wary of venomous snakes. Perhaps, then, speaking, toolmaking and snake-fearing humans survived for longer and had proportionally more offspring. Perhaps these descendants, faced with similar environmental challenges, developed similar aptitudes. But does this warrant the conclusion that these aptitudes, having evolved under the environmental conditions of the Pleistocene, were eventually so fixed in the human constitution that they are still in place today? Do contemporary human beings, without exception, carry the same general-purpose design? Is every human new-born pre-fitted with a device for acquiring language, a facility for designing and making his or her own tools and an automatic snake alarm?

It is undoubtedly true that the vast majority of human beings, beyond infancy, are capable of both speech and toolmaking. It may well be, too, that most people are afraid of snakes, even people like me who have rarely encountered them in real life save behind the glass of a reptilarium. We do seem to be a great deal more fearful of snakes than of guns or automobiles, even though in today's world, the chances of being harmed by the latter are hugely greater than by the former. So when I wake in panic from a snake-riddled nightmare, is that my alarm going off, a distant echo of the real experience of my earliest ancestors? Is there, subconsciously lurking inside every one of us, a hunter-gatherer struggling to get out? Are we, in short, the creatures of our evolutionary past, abroad in the present, fated to meet the challenges of twenty-first-century life with adaptations inherited from the Stone Age? It is still common to attribute many of the ills of civilization to the mismatch between the two. For example, an instinctive liking for sweet foods that would have been adaptive so long as supplies in nature were limited has been widely blamed for soaring rates of obesity and diabetes in the sugar-saturated nutritional environments of today. And displays of aggression, which for ancestral hunter-gatherers might have been relatively harmless ways of resolving conflict but can now be harnessed to fast-moving vehicles or ballistic missiles, have been blamed for everything from road-rage to the imminent threat of thermonuclear war.

This appeal to instinct, however, is fundamentally flawed, for one simple reason. A characteristic such as a sweet tooth, or a tendency for aggression (among males), or even a fear of snakes, is not something anyone is born with. It develops. At whatever point in the life-cycle it might be identified – whether in early or late childhood, youth, adulthood or old age – it arises through a process of growth and maturation within a certain environment. Technically, this process is known as *ontogenesis*. There is no attribute, capacity or disposition, in human beings as in creatures of any other kind, which has not arisen in the course of ontogenetic development. Once again, as with the idea of genetic determination, to attribute what we do to instinct is to read the outcome of a developmental process as its cause. In real life the conditions encountered in the environment play as formative a role in ontogenesis as anything intrinsic to the individuals in question. This is not to prioritize 'nurture' over 'nature'. It is not to say that human beings are fashioned by the environment *rather than* by their genes, nor even that we could factor out the respective contributions of each or weight them with percentages. No more than other living creatures are human beings the products of an interaction between interior and exterior causes, genes and environment. They are not products, period. They are the producers of their lives, responding at every moment to the conditions they encounter – conditions cumulatively shaped by their own and others' actions in the past.

We cannot therefore think of human differences as added on, thanks to environmental experience, to a baseline of universals that we have in common from the start. Human life is not a passage from uniformity to diversity, or, as it is often expressed, from nature to culture. Take language, for example. Whilst the vast majority of mature human beings share the gift of speech, their ways of speaking are extraordinarily varied. Many linguists have argued that this variation is made possible by the pre-installation, in the mind, of a so-called 'language acquisition device' (LAD) common to all. Humans have even been credited with a 'language instinct'.[5] But where has the LAD come from? To say it is 'in the genes' is to commit to a logic that we have already shown to be circular. A mental apparatus for acquiring language, were such a thing to exist, could only emerge in the course of early development. In practice, however, the human infant develops in an environment already saturated with the characteristic speech sounds of the community. These are sounds, especially of the mother's voice, that the infant hears long before it is even born: indeed they are the sounds of hearing itself as it develops for the foetus in the womb. It is impossible, therefore, to separate out the development of an 'innate' capacity for acquiring language in general from the 'learned' capacity to speak in the particular language or languages acquired thereby, as if the former preceded and laid the groundwork for the latter. Differentiation is there from the start.

Learning to speak, in short, *is* learning to speak in the way of one's people; it is not to add one layer, of linguistic particulars, on to another, of pre-established universals. The same goes for any other capabilities which we might select for attention. Thus, people learn to walk in many different ways, depending on the quality of the ground, the composition of footwear (if used), and variable expectations of what is proper for persons of different age, gender and status. But these differences are not added on to a universal capacity for bipedal locomotion somehow installed from the off. Your learning to walk is learning to walk in the way you do – a process, moreover, that is never completed but continues through life, in response partly to the support and company of others, and partly to the changing biodynamics of a body that is ever growing older. My father used to say that he began as a quadruped, evolving first into a biped, then, with walking stick, into a tripod, and finally, equipped with Zimmer frame, into an insect-like hexapod. These changes in motility were not imprinted upon his body but grown into it – into its very *modus operandi* – through practice and training in an environment. Thus embodiment and ontogenesis, the acquisition of particular techniques and the development of the human organism, are not set apart on opposite sides of a division between cultural conditioning and biological growth. They are one and the same. Our bodies are us, and we them. As they age, we do too.

The fashioning of human beings in the carrying on of life is a never-ending task. We are forever creating ourselves and one another. Our word for this process of collective self-fashioning is *history*. We make ourselves historically by establishing, in the things we do, the conditions under which generations to follow will grow to maturity. As these conditions change, so we do too. We develop attributes, capacities and dispositions unknown to our predecessors. Think of all the things we can do only thanks to the historical invention of the wheel. One is to ride a bicycle. Cycling is a bodily skill, nowadays so widely distributed that we think it almost as natural that human beings can ride as that they can walk. It can only develop, however, if the necessary conditions are in place, including a machine, tracks navigable on two wheels and someone – usually a parent – to get us started. We can lose capacities too, when the conditions for their development are no longer present. Even today, a generation of children is growing up who lack the ability to write by hand. In our digital age, handwriting has ceased to be regarded as a necessary life-skill. There may even come a time when future generations lose the capacity to walk; for astronauts the risk is already present. Thus it is a great mistake to populate the past and the future with people just like ourselves. Constitutionally, our distant descendants will not be the same as us, just as we are not constitutionally the same as our ancestors of long ago.

History, then, does not stand like an edifice on the pedestal of an evolved human nature. Most attempts to spell out this nature turn out on closer inspection to be but thinly disguised portraits of what their authors, steeped in the values of modernity, take to be the ideal accomplishments of humanity, including things like art, technology, science and reason. Projecting onto our hunter-gatherer ancestors the capacities to do everything we can do today, allegedly installed with the genetic capital of the species, history itself is made out to be the glorious process by which these capacities have been triumphantly fulfilled. Thus it is claimed that paintings preserved on the walls of caves, dating to around 30,000 years ago, reveal a capacity for art that culminated in the European Renaissance, that stone tools of the same period and provenance reveal a capacity for technology that has reached its peak with the microchip, that the people who made the paintings and the tools had the capacity to be a Newton or an Einstein. But this decidedly Eurocentric vision, popularly rendered as 'the ascent of man', casts aside the accomplishments of those whose histories happen not to fall in with the modern myth of progress. While attributing what we can do that they cannot to the greater development, in ourselves, of capacities universal to the species, it relegates whatever they can do that we cannot to the peculiarities of cultural tradition. Human nature, then, serves as little more than a prop to support the belief in our own superiority.

Like most people born and brought up in a nominally 'western' society, I am used to sitting on chairs but find squatting acutely uncomfortable. I can walk but cannot balance loads on my head (see Figure 2). I can read and write but have no memory for epic storytelling. What, apart from the bias of my upbringing, prevents me from acknowledging squatting, carrying on the head and storytelling as species-wide aptitudes more fully developed among people of other civilizations than in my own? The only way to overcome this bias would be to bring all such aptitudes under the umbrella of a generalized capacity to do everything that human beings have ever done in the past and that their successors will ever do in the future. In the idiom of anthropology, this has been called a 'capacity for culture'.

Figure 2 Women carrying bundles of eucalyptus branches on their heads, down the slopes of the Entoto hills near Addis Ababa, Ethiopia. They will sell the wood in the city, for use in cooking. A sketch by Manuel Ramos, courtesy of the artist-ethnographer.

The argument goes that while forms of human life may vary virtually without limit, the capacity to acquire these forms is common to all – a true universal with which all human beings are equipped from the start. Humans, it is supposed, are naturally pre-programmed to acquire the culture of the community into which they are born, just as they are to acquire its language. Unlike other animals that know instinctively how to do things, human beings have to learn. Starved of opportunities to do so, an individual would be left stunted and crippled. Uniquely for humans, then, culture is alleged to make up the deficit between what nature gives us and what we need in order to function in the world.

This was the thinking behind an oft-repeated verdict on the human condition, pronounced some fifty years ago by the American anthropologist Clifford Geertz: 'One of the most significant facts about us', Geertz concluded, 'may finally be that we all begin with the natural equipment to live a thousand kinds of life but end in the end having lived only one.'[6] Human life, in this view, is a movement from the universal to the particular, from the naturally given to the culturally acquired, entailing a gradual filling up of capacities and narrowing down of possibilities. Our verdict, however, is precisely the reverse. It is that life is a movement not of closure but of opening, which continually overtakes any ends that might be placed before it. Thus our equipment for life, including techniques of the body and habits of the mind, is not ready-made but continually forged in the crucible of activities conducted with or alongside others. Children's abilities to walk and talk, for example, develop in growing bodies amidst

43

countless attempts to get moving, to keep up with their fellows, draw their attention and make themselves understood. If most humans grow up walking and talking, it is not because the abilities to do both are undergirded by capacities given from the start, but because their improvisations in movement and communication – under a range of environmental conditions and with the support of companions – tend to converge. It is in these convergences, and not in what people have in common to begin with, that the answer to the question of human nature lies.

Human lives do not, then, begin united in nature and end divided by culture. There has to be something wrong with any explanatory scheme that needs to base itself on the ludicrous claim – in the words of evolutionary psychologists John Tooby and Leda Cosmides – that 'infants are everywhere the same'.[7] Every infant is different, not just because of its unique genome, but because each comes into the world in a certain place, at a certain time, having already undergone a formative period of gestation in the womb of the mother-to-be, herself immersed in the life of her community and engaged with its environment. Each of us, launched into this world of continuous variation, has no alternative but to carry on from then and there, cutting a course which – rather like the stream of a river delta – is ever converging with and diverging from the lifeways of others. Convergence and divergence proceed hand in hand for the duration of the life-cycle; thus we are no more different from one another, as we approach the end of life, than we were the same when we were born. Throughout life, from cradle to grave, people differentiate themselves from one another in the very process of going along together. In the human family, for example, the lives of siblings who had once shared the intimacy of home and hearth fan out, only to merge with other lives in the foundation of families of their own. It is their sameness that divides. Difference, on the contrary, is the glue that binds us all.

If this is the lesson of anthropology today, it is not what I was taught as an undergraduate student of anthropology at the University of Cambridge some fifty years ago! In those days it went without saying that difference meant division. It was about being able to tell things or people apart, which you could only do by assigning them to categories, of this kind or that, at higher or lower levels of resolution. Thus animal kinds, distinguished at the species level, might be grouped as of the same genus. And people who, at one level, would categorize themselves by what they do in common, as against those who do things differently, would, at another level, sink their differences and unite with these others against those yet further removed. This ordering of the world into nested segments was drummed into us as something approaching a law of anthropology. One of my teachers at that time was Edmund Leach, who besides being a distinguished social anthropologist was also a prominent public intellectual. In 1967, Leach delivered the BBC Reith Lectures under the title *A Runaway World?* It is a fact about the human condition, he declared in one of his lectures, that all difference is contrastive. Thus '*I* identify myself with a collective *we* which is then contrasted with some *other*.'[8] There can be no 'us', Leach told his audience, without a 'them'. We are the same in doing this, they are the same in doing that; in a divided world, difference is pushed onto the boundary between them and us.

Is this where identity lies – in what makes us all the same, or identical? Does identity mark us out as members of an in-group? Does difference lie at the outer fringes of identity, or at its heart? These questions are among the most troublesome of our age. For they touch on the very foundations of our place in the world, of who we think we are. Ask me who I am, and I can fully answer only by telling my story. It would be a story about the relationships I have enjoyed, in the course of my life so far, with the people around me, the places I have inhabited, and the things I have made and used. It is to them that I owe my existence, and they also, to some measure, owe their existence to me. Your story, of course, will be different from mine, yet as surely as you are reading these lines, we are also fellow travellers through the landscape of social relations. In a topographic landscape, a person can walk from place to place without crossing any boundary. Is it not, then, equally possible for a place to pass from person to person – that is, for them to establish a *commonplace* – without surrendering their difference to a bland similarity? If you and I and all the rest of us were already the same, what would we have to talk about? What kind of conversation could we have? Only because we bring different things to the table – experiences, observations, skills – can they become matters in common.

Indeed the very term 'community', from the Latin *com* ('together') plus *munus* ('gift'), means not just 'living together' but 'giving together'. We belong to communities because each of us, being different, has something to give. Identity in community is thus fundamentally *relational*: who we are is an index of where we find ourselves, at any moment, in the give and take of collective life. This sense of identity, however, is strikingly at odds with the constitution of the modern state, which tolerates no difference among its citizens but rather demands equality in obligation and entitlement. Identity, for the citizen, is not about belonging to others, to community or to place. It is rather an *attribute* that belongs to you, a right or possession that you own, and that can even be stolen. The potentially explosive charge of the concept of identity, and its capacity to wreak political havoc, lies precisely in the contradiction between these two senses, respectively relational and attributional. It is a contradiction that tends to emerge whenever the community feels itself under threat from the power of the state. At such times, people are called upon to assert their difference in attributional terms. This is to recast the very relationships from which they derive their sense of belonging as the outward expressions of inner, inherited properties that belong to them. It is to turn the 'we' of the community into 'people like us', united against 'them' in the defence of a shared heritage or cultural essence. Herein lie the roots of the phenomenon of ethnicity.

But if 'we' are the community, then who are 'they'? If we belong, they do not; if we owe our existence to others, they do not; if we have a place in the world, they do not; if we have stories to tell, they do not. Who are these people, at once beholden to no-one, inhabitants of nowhere and committed to universality in thought and expression? They are, of course, the archetypal representatives of modernity, citizens of what we call 'the West'. One of the paradoxes of anthropology is that while it has much to say about the lives and times of non-western peoples, it has next to nothing to say about the people of the West. For the most part, the West is invoked as a foil against which to contrast the particularity of experience for people living someplace, sometime. It is 'the outside world', 'the wider society' or simply 'the majority'. Even the inhabitants of nominally western countries, such as Britain or the United States, appear thoroughly non-western under the anthropological lens. Westerners, it turns out, are always conspicuous by their absence. For in truth, they have never existed. Despite strident assertions of the universal values of modernity, by philosophers and statesmen alike, it is not practicably possible to live by them. Cosmopolitan, rational and uncompromisingly self-interested, belonging nowhere and to no-one, the modern westerner is a figment of our imagination. Or as philosopher Bruno Latour put it in the title of a celebrated book, 'we have never been modern'.[9] Who, then, are the 'we' of his title?

49

Similarity and Difference

We cannot be westerners if such characters do not exist. Nor can we be non-westerners if there are none to which we are opposed. Perhaps you will say we are human beings, but that would only make us all alike in our species-wide opposition to non-humans. A relational approach to identity, however, opens up a radically *non-oppositional* understanding of what 'we' could mean – an understanding that would allow us, at long last, to escape the self-perpetuating polarization of the West and the rest, and indeed of humanity and nature. Rather than rebounding inwards from a frontier between all who are like me and all who are not, 'we', in this sense, reaches without limit from where I am currently positioned into the landscape of relations. It neither includes nor excludes but *spreads*. It is a search for common ground, not the defence of existing heritage. It exposes us to others rather than conferring immunity from contact with them. This 'we' is a community of relations bound, but not bounded, by difference. Here, difference and similarity, becoming other and coming together, go hand in hand. And if, at the end of the day, we inhabit but one world, it is because this world, too, is neither the natural preserve of a global humanity nor a flatbed of universals but a field of infinite and ever-emerging historical variation. It is to the inhabitants of this world, whatever their provenance, that I address the question with which I began this book: 'How should we live?' For they are us, the 'we' of anthropology.

3

A Discipline Divided

I was supposed to become a scientist. But as I commenced my university studies, in 1966, it began to dawn on me that something was terribly amiss with science. Ostensibly committed to principles of openness, and to the advance of knowledge for the benefit of all humanity, science – at least in the way it was taught to us – had become stultified, intellectually claustrophobic and dedicated to the regimented and narrow-minded pursuit of objectives remote from experience. At that time the war in Vietnam was at its height, and many of my fellow students were outraged by science's apparent renunciation of its democratic principles and its surrender to the megamachines of industrial and military power. I, too, was offended by the evident refusal of scientific institutes to shoulder any responsibility for the ways their research was applied: for them it was always a matter for others, be they politicians, military men or captains of industry. What most bothered me, however, was the sheer hubris permeating the scientific establishment. There was no problem for which science could not engineer a technological solution. To the suffering of those most directly exposed to the chemical, carcinogenic and radioactive fallout of scientific progress, the response was invariably that science could be relied upon to find the cures. In those days the issue of global warming was scarcely on the horizon. But the attitude of arrogant self-confidence has persisted among prophets of geoengineering convinced that the entire earth can be fixed for the benefit of humanity, heralding a new age of total planetary control.

At the other end of the spectrum were scholars in various disciplines of the humanities. They, to my impatient student eyes, appeared to be afflicted by an astonishing complacency. With their heads buried in libraries and archives, sunk in the esoterica of worlds long gone, they, too, seemed ill prepared to address the urgency of the contemporary human condition. It seemed that for them, anything coming too close to the realities of life, as experienced today, was too hot to handle. Between these scholars and the scientists there persisted a mutual standoff. Scarcely a word passed between

53

them. Reflecting on this, I became convinced that the division between the natural sciences and the humanities, which seemed only to be widening, was the great tragedy of the intellectual history of the West. As with all tragedies, the division had unfolded with a certain inevitability, underwritten by the very excision of humanity from nature, and of ways of knowing the world from ways of being in it, that has been a hallmark of the western tradition of thought from classical times. As we have seen, it is rooted in our very conception of the human. Though only a vague intuition when I began my university studies, it was the sense of foreboding that this could end only with humanity's self-destruction which eventually drew me to anthropology. Here was a discipline, I thought, that existed to bring the two sides together again, to reunite the human being with being human, yet in a way that never loses sight of lived experience.

Thus it came to pass that, after a frustrating year of reading natural science at university, I switched to anthropology. Since then, I have never looked back. I have, however, looked with increasing concern from side to side, only to see the discipline riven by the very divisions I had thought it existed to overcome. There are scholars who call themselves social or cultural anthropologists, or, just as often, ethnographers. And there are scholars who call themselves physical or biological anthropologists, or, just as often, students of human evolution. The former are conversant with other fields of the humanities, from philosophical and literary studies to history and comparative religion. The latter hold court with evolutionary psychologists, neuroscientists, behavioural ecologists and palaeontologists. Rarely, however, do they speak with one another, and if they do it is only to rediscover the depth of their antipathy. To further complicate the picture, all sorts of other anthropologies have emerged over recent decades, each with its own interests, ways of working and publication outlets. There are – in no particular order – medical anthropologists, visual anthropologists, environmental anthropologists, cognitive anthropologists, development anthropologists, design anthropologists, urban anthropologists, historical anthropologists, forensic anthropologists, cyber anthropologists. Scholars who identify as anthropologists also work in fields of study that do not have 'anthropology' in their titles: material culture studies, museum studies, science and technology studies. For the novice, this variety can be bewildering. Has the discipline finally exploded into so many ill-fitting fragments that, like Humpty-Dumpty, it can never be reassembled?

Behind all these anthropologies, is there anything to hold them together?

I could not write a book on anthropology and why it matters unless I believed there is, at least potentially, something that binds these proliferating threads into a whole rope. But to get at what it might be, we need first to take a step back, to join the anthropological conversation in its inception and follow its subsequent ups and downs. That will be my task in this chapter. It is important to understand why anthropology began as it did, with the imperious ambition to forge a unified 'science of man', and why, eventually, it fell apart. To rebuild anthropology for the future, we need to learn the lessons of the past. These are not always affirmative. Most scholarly disciplines are proud of their pasts: they like to celebrate their illustrious ancestors, men of vision who laid the foundations for great things to come. Their wigged and bearded countenances adorn the pages of textbooks. But anthropology is not so fortunate. Our ancestors were a mixed bunch, including a fair number of visionaries, crackpots, racists and bigots. Our cupboards are literally full of skeletons, not to mention everything from shrunken heads to ritual paraphernalia, stolen from peoples from around the world to fill our museums. We are not proud of the crew of skull-measurers, treasure-hunters and culture-thieves who fill the pages of a disciplinary history that reads more like a series of false starts than a race to the finish. In the public understanding of anthropology, we are still stalked by a past that most of us would prefer to forget.

Like many disciplines in the modern academic pantheon, anthropology is a child of the Age of Reason. It grew up amidst the ferment of ideas that accompanied the rejection of religious dogma and political despotism by liberal philosophers and intellectuals of the seventeenth and eighteenth centuries. They were the leading lights of the movement that became known, in the history of European thought, as the Enlightenment. Committed to ideals of rational inquiry, spiritual tolerance and individual liberty, Enlightenment thinkers saw it as their great civilizing mission to emancipate humanity from superstition and dogma. This was a noble calling, but it had a flipside. For the master-narrative of civilization had to begin somewhere. It had to conjecture an original condition from which the great ascent of humanity could commence. To be raised to civilization, humans must once have been primitive. This led to much speculation on what life in this original state of nature might have been like. 'Nasty, brutish and short' was the famous conclusion of Thomas Hobbes, who effectively launched the English Enlightenment. His fellow countryman, John Locke, wondered at what point a man who draws sustenance from Nature might be said, unlike wild beasts, to have 'begun a Property' over what he takes. On the other side of the Channel, in France, Jean-Jacques Rousseau eulogized the equality and self-esteem (*amour propre*) of the natural man or savage, while in Scotland, Adam Ferguson reflected on what it meant to have renounced the savage's autonomous liberty for the civil liberty enjoyed by men of reason.

For the most part, these speculations were unconstrained by evidence. The savage was an invention of erudite European minds, fleshed out to various degrees with often lurid travellers' tales of native life in the Americas, and in the colonial territories then being established in Africa, the East Indies and Australia. At that time, the full range of human variation was not yet known, and debate raged over whether the inhabitants of some of these lands were really human beings at all. It was the great Swedish naturalist Carolus Linnaeus who took the momentous step – considered outrageous by many of his contemporaries – of placing human beings, under the genus *Homo*, in the order of Primates, within a scheme of classification that encompassed the entire animal kingdom. But there was little

Figure 3 'Anthropomorpha', from Christian Emmanuel Hoppius, *Amoenitates academicae* (1763). Lucifer is the second figure from the left.

agreement on what the distinguishing marks of this genus might be. Reports were coming in, for example, of anthropomorphic creatures with tails. Could they be human? The eccentric Scottish judge James Burnett, alias Lord Monboddo, argued that they could. In the first of six volumes entitled *Of the Origin and Progress of Language*, published in 1773, Monboddo commented on an engraving he had seen in a treatise of Linnaeus, depicting human types (see Figure 3). One, christened Lucifer, sported a tail. Monboddo was happy to accept Lucifer as a human being. Anticipating the incredulity of his readers, he warned them not to be bound by their own, familiar ideas of what humans were like. Just because they had never met humans with tails did not mean that such creatures could not exist.

Monboddo was wrong: anatomically, humans have no tails. It transpired that Lucifer had been copied from a work of the sixteenth-century naturalist Ulisse Aldrovandi, and the draughtsman – a pupil of Linnaeus by the name of Hoppius – reckoned it depicted one of a fabled tribe of cat-tailed cannibals. But perhaps Monboddo was wrong for the right reasons. As for Linnaeus, he had concluded that one could only tell humans apart by asking them. Apes and humans may look alike – neither have tails – but only humans can see themselves for what they are. This, thought Linnaeus, is because they have been endowed, by their Creator, not only with a functioning body but also with the gift of intellect or reason: that is, with a *mind*. There are no philosophers among the apes. Yet the question remained: could this mind be improved, could its possessors be raised from savagery to civilization, within the compass of a constant anatomical form? Were the brain and body pre-designed to hold the weight of learning? Could mental advance even lead to improvements in bodily physique? One who believed it could was Robert Fitzroy, captain of HMS *Beagle*. On one occasion, while his ship was moored off the island of Tierra del Fuego at the southernmost tip of South America, a party of four natives chanced to find themselves on board. Fitzroy resolved there and then to take them back to England to be trained in the manners of the country. After some years he would return them to their native land to spread the word.

On board the *Beagle* for the return journey, again under Fitzroy's command, was the young Charles Darwin. Darwin formed a favourable impression of his 'Fuegian' travelling companions, whose mental powers, he deemed, were not vastly inferior to his own. They were well-dressed, well-mannered and affable. But when the *Beagle* arrived back in Tierra del Fuego, in December 1832, Darwin was in for a shock. So unkempt were the natives encountered there, he remarked, that he could scarcely believe they were human beings like himself. Never, in his estimation, had he come across creatures in a more abject condition. The account in his journal is peppered with such words as 'stunted', 'hideous', 'filthy', 'greasy' and 'violent'. Of language, there was nothing but clicks and grunts; of moral sense or civility, none. The experience of the encounter is one Darwin never forgot. Writing four decades later, in *The Descent of Man*, he still recalled the moment when, on first setting eyes on a party of natives on the Fuegian shore, the thought had rushed into his mind: were our ancestors such as these? Would we not rather be descended from monkeys or baboons? Surely, he mused, these wretched souls must represent the lowest state of man to be found anywhere on earth. Yet he took their very debasement to lend strength to his argument, namely that the gap between the human and animals lower in the scale is so narrow as to be readily bridged, and, moreover, that it is no different, in principle, from that which separates the wild and the civilized man.

The Descent of Man was published in 1871. In it, Darwin sought to extend to humankind the principles he had already set forth in his earlier work, *On the Origin of Species*. The attempt was not without contradiction. Where the *Origin* was all about how organic bodies of diverse kinds come to be adapted to their variable conditions of life, without presupposing any necessary advance from lower to higher forms, the *Descent* was above all about the progress of the mind, without regard to specific environmental conditions, from its most elementary manifestations in the lowliest of animals to its heights in human civilization. Darwin was convinced that powers of intelligence we recognize in ourselves are not limited to humans but traverse the entire gamut of animal kinds. Even the lowly earthworm, he thought, is possessed of a rudimentary intelligence. In closing the gap between humans and animals, then, Darwin was not downgrading humans so much as upgrading animals. In fact Thomas Henry Huxley – zoologist, palaeontologist and staunch Darwinian – beat Darwin into print on this point. In an essay on 'Man's place in nature', published in 1863, Huxley declared not only that no absolute line of demarcation separates ourselves from other animals, but also that what goes for physical characteristics goes as well for mental ones – indeed, as he put it, 'the highest faculties of feeling and intellect begin to germinate in lower forms of life'.[1] In Huxley's vivid metaphor, civilization has sprung from bestial origins as surely as Alpine peaks are raised up from the mud of ancient seas.

What force is capable of driving up civilization from the sludge of bestiality? For Darwin as for Huxley, the answer was not in doubt. It was, of course, natural selection. In the incessant struggle for existence, as Darwin was wont to put it, the more intelligent would always emerge victorious, supplanting their weaker-witted competitors. Over time, intelligence-enhancing variations would tend to be preserved, ratcheting up across the generations so as to bring about general advance. Critically, however, this argument could only work on one condition, namely that the variations in question are heritable and in that sense innate. The effects of inserting this condition into the thinking of the time cannot be overestimated. The 1860s and 1870s had seen the publication of a spate of scholarly treatises which sought to chart human progress in fields of law and custom, marriage and the family, religion and belief, and economic life, through a determinate series of stages. They included such classics as Henry Maine's *Ancient Law*, Lewis Henry Morgan's *Ancient Society*, John Ferguson McLennan's *Primitive Marriage*, Johann Jakob Bachofen's *Mother Right* and Edward Burnett Tylor's *Primitive Culture*. All, however, were founded on the doctrine – attributed to the German polymath Adolf Bastian – of the 'psychic unity of mankind'. According to this doctrine, human beings are equally and universally endowed with the faculty of mind, differing from nation to nation only in the extent of its cultivation. It was as if so-called 'savage', 'barbarous' and 'civilized' nations represented successive stages of advance – introductory, intermediate and advanced – through a core curriculum common to humankind.

But between them, Darwin and Huxley managed to lay a fuse that threatened to blow up the entire, carefully constructed edifice. For it opened the door to those who believed that the best way to secure human improvement, across the board, was to give nature a helping hand by hastening the demise of those whose mental endowments were considered inferior: the poor, the indigent, people of non-white races. In later years this belief would come to be known – principally by its opponents – as 'social Darwinism'. Darwin's own cousin, Francis Galton, was instrumental in founding the eugenics movement, dedicated to the artificial improvement of the human race through controlled selective breeding. To his credit, Darwin himself never suggested anything so drastic. He was no Darwinist. Nevertheless, he was firmly of the view that efforts to secure lasting improvement through education – such as Captain Fitzroy's abortive adventure with the Fuegians – were doomed to failure. In the grand drama of the rise of civilization through the struggle for existence, set out in the pages of *The Descent of Man*, savages were destined not to emerge victorious but to play the role of the vanquished. For Darwin's many readers, the book provided a convenient narrative, apparently backed by scientific authority, which at once accounted for the entitlement of people of European descent to inherit the earth, and justified the adventures of colonization and genocide wreaked upon populations beyond the continent. Eventually, this narrative would condense around a single word, one of the most incendiary in the recent history of ideas. That word was 'evolution'.

The discipline of anthropology was reborn in the explosion. From the late nineteenth century and beyond, anthropology mattered to its public above all because it promised a unified account of human evolution. This evolution was understood to proceed on three fronts: anatomical, artefactual and institutional. Each was to be studied by a different branch of the discipline. Physical anthropologists studied the evolution of human anatomy, and above all of the skull, seat of the brain and of human intelligence. Archaeologists studied the evolution of tools, buildings and other artefacts. And social or cultural anthropologists studied the evolution of institutions, customs and beliefs. Herein lay the origin of what is often called the 'three-field' makeup of anthropology, enshrined, for example, in the constitution of one of its most venerable bodies, the Royal Anthropological Institute of Great Britain and Ireland, founded in that fateful year of 1871 which also saw the publication of *The Descent of Man*. The idea was that anatomical types, artefactual assemblages and institutional forms could eventually be integrated into an overarching typological sequence, running from the most primitive to the most advanced. Many leading anthropological museums were established in the same period, dedicated to the public demonstration of this sequence. In them, materials collected from dispersed peoples or places were gathered together according to their level of culture. But this also meant dispersing the materials from each place or people into separate typological compartments. As visitors proceeded around the gallery, the whole panoply of human evolution, in all its facets, would unfold before their eyes.

One enthusiastic advocate of the three-field approach was Robert Reid, Professor of Anatomy at the University of Aberdeen, in northeast Scotland, and founding curator of the University's anthropological museum. Reid compulsively measured up and classified everyone he could find, in the name of an anthropology conceived as the 'science of man'. He studied the relation between head size and intelligence, publishing his results in the Royal Anthropological Institute's journal. And he trained his disciples to go out into the world and collect data on the characteristics of the 'white or Caucasian, the yellow and red Mongolian, the Australian, and Frizzly-haired or Black Races'.[2] Reid's polychrome litany of racial types, however, was nothing compared with the pronouncements of a far more influential Aberdonian, who also began as an anatomist but devoted much of his career to anthropology. Sir Arthur Keith, knight of the realm, one-time President of the Royal Anthropological Institute, and latterly Rector of the University of Aberdeen, was among the most established scientific figures of his day. In his Rectorial Address of 1931, Keith scorned the idea that the nations of the world could ever be united in brotherhood. Prejudice and xenophobia, Keith argued, work for the good of mankind. Loyalty to one's own race and hatred of others constitute the very engine of evolutionary progress. Far from mixing bloods of different colours – white, yellow, brown and black – it is imperative to keep them separate, leaving it to nature to ensure that only the brightest colours are retained. The war of races, Keith declared, is Nature's pruning hook.[3]

This kind of racial thinking was alive and well in the anthropology of the interwar period. It took the second war to break out in a century among the supposedly civilized races of Europe, itself fuelled by xenophobic hatred, finally to lay it to rest. In the wake of the Holocaust, what had been the bedrock assumption of evolutionary science since Darwin and Huxley – that human populations differ in their intellectual capacities on a scale from primitive to civilized – was no longer tenable. In its stead was planted a firm ethical commitment to the principle that *all* humans, whether alive in the past, present or future, are equal in their moral and intellectual capacities. 'All human beings', as Article 1 of the Universal Declaration of Human Rights states, 'are endowed with reason and conscience.' To emphasize this unity, scientists reclassified extant human beings as members not just of the same species but of the same sub-species, designated *Homo sapiens sapiens*. Doubly sapient, the first attribution of wisdom – the outcome of increasing brain size and complexity – marks humans out within the world of living beings. But the second, far from marking a further subdivision, registers their decisive break from that world. With this break, unparalleled in the history of life, humanity is supposed to have been set on the road to civilization. Thenceforth, our ancestors found themselves on both sides of the fence: both in nature and out of it. And it is with this cast of hybrid characters that the evolutionary anthropology of the later twentieth century populated the planet.

What, then, was left of the three-field approach? Many contemporary anthropologists would answer that nothing remains, and that the continued coexistence of the three branches of anthropology under the same roof, in a handful of universities, is an anachronistic hangover from the discipline's unsavoury past. One of these institutions was the University of Cambridge, which is why I found myself, in my first year of studying anthropology, taking courses in physical anthropology, archaeology and social anthropology. I recall classes in physical anthropology in which I was taught to identify human types from nude photographs of men and women from around the world, and to measure the dimensions from the casts of fossil skulls. In archaeology we learned how to recognize stone artefacts, and assign them to categories indicative of successive stages of prehistory. But social anthropology was quite different. It was, we were told, essentially a social science, and our bible was a slim volume, entitled *Structure and Function in Primitive Society*, by the self-styled founder of the sub-discipline in its modern form, Alfred Reginald Radcliffe-Brown. In it, we were informed that social anthropology is a branch of comparative sociology dealing specifically with primitive societies.[4] Having completed my foundation year, I had to choose between physical anthropology, archaeology and social anthropology for continuing study, and I selected social anthropology. While I had gained much from studying the other two, it was already apparent that they were out of kilter: that physical anthropology and, to a lesser extent, archaeology were still clinging to an evolutionary approach that social anthropology had unequivocally rejected.

The split dates back to the interwar years, and had much to do with the ways in which anthropologists of different persuasions would obtain their evidence. For both physical anthropology and archaeology, most of the evidence lies underground, in the form of fossilized remains, ancient burials and lithic deposits. It can only be revealed through excavation. But you cannot dig up the whole world, and a lot depends on guesswork, accident and sheer good fortune. Social anthropologists, however, faced a problem more intractable than the paucity of evidence. Simply, customs and institutions do not preserve like bones and stones, and you cannot dig them up. How, then, can their evolution possibly be demonstrated? Confronted with this problem, the only solution was to assume that all social evolution passes through the same stages. Following from this assumption, the lifeways of peoples deemed to be 'primitive' could be seen to offer a window on the earlier social condition of humans in general. It was as though to travel in space to remote corners of the world – to the jungles of Africa, the deserts of

Australia, the Arctic tundra – was also to travel back in time, to a remote epoch in the social evolution of humanity. Their present becomes the model for our past. Indeed the idea that so-called 'primitive tribes' – or what might today be known, more politely, as 'indigenous peoples' – are living fossils, surviving remnants of an era long since overtaken by the modern world and destined for disappearance, continues to colour the ways they are represented in public media.

But however persistent this kind of thinking may be in the popular imagination, it had long since been refuted within social anthropology. In the 1920s and 1930s it came under sustained attack from anthropologists who argued for a quite different approach to social and cultural phenomena. Instead of trying to show how customs and institutions originated and evolved, they said, we should be trying to show how they work. That is, we should show how – for those present-day people who practise the customs and maintain the institutions – they actually serve a purpose, whether to satisfy the given needs of individual human beings or to secure the continuity of the total society to which they belong. This approach came to be known as *functionalism*. The functionalists had no time for evolutionary reconstructions which, in the absence of written records, they regarded as purely conjectural. Since we cannot know how customs and institutions actually evolved, they argued, we would do better to attend to what actually matters to people: not where the practices in question came from but their current purpose and utility. A tool or technique, for example, only has meaning as it is used in the context of an ongoing way of life. What are tools without the skills to use them? Artefacts may preserve, but skills don't. The American cultural anthropologist Marshall Sahlins cites the aphorism of an unnamed but allegedly reputable archaeologist: 'the people, they're dead'.[5] Only artefacts remain. For Sahlins, that was enough to write off the entire mission of archaeology to reconstruct the lineages of ancient technology.

More than anything, the rise of functionalism led social anthropology to split off from its sister fields of physical anthropology and archaeology, which continued with their evolutionary orientation. There was, however, another reason for the split, which went back to the vexed question of the relation between race and culture. This had been a grey area for decades, with many allowing that characteristics acquired in life could be transmitted to offspring as an innate endowment. The doctrine known as the 'inheritance of acquired characteristics', often (and incorrectly) attributed to Jean-Baptiste Lamarck – naturalist and originator of the term 'biology' – was not finally refuted until the close of the nineteenth century, and it took a couple of decades more for its implications to filter through to anthropology. They were, simply, that race and culture, biological heredity and the heritage of tradition, had to be kept strictly separate. It became part of anthropological orthodoxy to declare that any child born of man and woman, whatever their biological ancestry, could just as readily acquire one form of cultural life as another. A person born of Chinese parents but transported in infancy to France, and adopted by French parents, would – in physical appearance – look unmistakably Chinese, but would in comportment and behaviour be thoroughly French. This finally drove the wedge between physical or biological anthropology, on the one hand, and social or cultural anthropology, on the other. One could study the biological variation of humankind, or one could study cultural variation, but these were separate enterprises that had nothing whatever to do with one another.

In 1917 Alfred Kroeber, one of the leading American anthropologists of the day, published an influential paper entitled 'The superorganic'.[6] In it, he spelled out the terms of a settlement between race and culture that would remain virtually intact for the remainder of the century. Culture, Kroeber declared, bears no more relation to heredity than a text to the tablet it is written on. It belongs to a realm of its own, over and above the organic. Significantly, however, Kroeber's focus was on culture, and not society. At that time, anthropology was developing along rather different lines in North America than in Britain. The difference came down to whether one's concern was with the ways people relate to one another in the conduct of social life, or with the traditions of knowledge and belief they carry with them and pass on to their descendants. Whilst in Britain, *social* anthropology was primarily concerned with the former, and thus conceived as a branch of sociology, its North American counterpart – namely *cultural* anthropology – was more concerned with the latter and was generally regarded as an offshoot of what was then called ethnology. The roots of ethnology lay in countries of continental Europe, where it had flourished around the turn of the twentieth century as the study of their indigenous 'folk' traditions, lending succour to the many nationalist movements springing up at the time. Even today, in these countries, cultural anthropology sometimes flies under the flag of ethnology, and where it does not it has had to distinguish itself as the study of exclusively *non*-European peoples.

But in North America, Europeans arrived as immigrants in a land already inhabited by people of a very different complexion. The scholar often celebrated as the father of American cultural anthropology, Franz Boas, himself emigrated to the United States, in 1887, having previously studied geography and physics in his native Germany. Initially convinced that human racial variation was not so much innate as environmentally conditioned, Boas was persuaded by the experience of ethnological research among Inuit people in the Canadian Arctic to substitute culture for race, heritage for heredity. Where racial variation is inscribed in the body, he reasoned, cultural variation is inscribed in the mind. Received as heritage rather than heredity, culture for Boas amounted to a legacy of tradition, passively absorbed rather than actively cultivated, which would shape the belief and practice of a people. Boas's prolific writings did much to establish cultural anthropology in North America, in the early decades of the twentieth century, and his many students, including Kroeber, went on to become leading voices in the new discipline. Kroeber, himself the son of immigrants from Germany, was thoroughly conversant with the Romantic tradition of German scholarship, with its emphasis on the diversity of folkways, the authenticity of feeling and the unity of man and nature. Indeed the influence of German Romanticism was one reason why American cultural anthropology took on such a different character compared with its British social anthropological counterpart, which remained wedded to ideas from the French and Scottish Enlightenment with its stress on civility, rationality and the transcendence of nature.

But there were historical as well as intellectual reasons for the divergence. Britain had its empire and turned to anthropology for guidance on native social institutions to help in the administration of colonial policy. America, by contrast, had its native populations, and needed anthropology to record ways of life fast disappearing. However, by the time I graduated in social anthropology, in 1970, the landscape of scholarship was fundamentally altered. With Britain's loss of empire, social anthropology had ceased to serve as the handmaiden of colonial rule, while in North America, as around the world, native peoples were finding their own voice in struggles for self-determination. In this transformed landscape, the distinction between social and cultural anthropology seemed increasingly irrelevant. Here, at least, there was convergence. But in other respects, anthropology was more divided than ever. In Britain the original three fields, once united under the banner of evolution, had gone their separate ways: physical anthropology to join evolutionary biology; prehistoric archaeology to join with classical archaeology as a discipline in its own right; social anthropology to join the social sciences. In America, anthropology had not three fields but four: cultural, archaeological, biological and linguistic. The reasons for the disappearance of the study of language from British anthropology are obscure, and need not detain us, but even in America, linguistic anthropology remained a minority specialism. And here, too, archaeology had gone its own way, while cultural and biological anthropologists, for the most part, were scarcely on speaking terms. Was anthropology, then, a discipline in ruins? To many, it seemed so.

4

Rethinking the Social

Remember Radcliffe-Brown? Few do today, except as a footnote, but as you will recall from the previous chapter, it was he who launched the field of social anthropology as a branch of sociology distinguished by its attention to primitive societies. Nowadays we tend to cringe at the word 'primitive', and do our best to avoid it, but not without a certain duplicity. For whenever we use words such as 'complex', 'large-scale' or 'modern' for societies like our own, we call to mind their opposites: societies which are simple, small-scale and traditional. And this, rather than any judgement of the powers or characteristics of the people who live in them, is what Radcliffe-Brown and his contemporaries implied by 'primitive'. Social anthropology, then, was conceived as the comparative study of the forms of life to be found in such societies. With a naturalist's eye, Radcliffe-Brown likened these forms to those of sea-shells. Combing the beach, one can find shells of all sorts, and these can be compared and classified into species and genera. Yet their fundamental forms appear to be limited: spiral such as the nautilus; radial such as the limpet; bivalvular such as the clam. Might it be the same for social as for organic forms? Might there be only a limited number of ways in which institutions could be assembled into a well-functioning society? If so, then systematic comparative analysis could reveal them. They are more readily revealed, moreover, by comparing small-scale societies rather than the large-scale societies studied by sociologists. This, for Radcliffe-Brown, was the task of social anthropology.

The idea of a comparative study of human societies sounds plausible, until you stop to ask what a society is. The trouble is that societies don't exist for anthropologists quite as organisms do for biologists. They are not entities you can see or touch. We think we all live in societies, indeed that we could scarcely live a human kind of life if we did not. But can you tell where your society ends and another begins, or at what moment it was born? What sense does it make to say of institutions that they function to maintain the society of which they are part, as organs maintain the living body, when in social life nothing ever stays the same even for a moment? As the ancient Greek philosopher Heraclitus is alleged to have said of the waters of a flowing river, you cannot step twice into the current of social life. Nothing repeats. Whenever you try to pin society down, social life runs through your fingers. In nature, one kind of animal does not become another – horses remain horses and do not turn into elephants – but in history transformations of this sort are going on continually. As Radcliffe-Brown himself acknowledged, the reality with which we deal, in social anthropological research, is not an entity but a process. But if that is so, then how can its forms be compared? Social life is one thing, the life of society another, and attempting to hold on to both at once is like squaring a circle. Radcliffe-Brown never managed to do so.

Indeed Edmund Leach, whom we encountered in Chapter 2 as the author of *A Runaway World?*, had nothing but contempt for Radcliffe-Brown's ambition to identify and compare the objective forms of society. It was, he scoffed, little better than butterfly-collecting.[1] Leach had come to anthropology from a background in engineering, so it is perhaps no wonder that he was inclined to liken the workings of society more to the operation of a mechanism than to the functioning of an organism. His method was to start not from observations of real life but from the drawing board. Imagine a machine with a limited number of dials, each of which controls for a particular variable and affords certain settings. Think of all the possible combinations of settings. Let us suppose, then, that every combination corresponds to a conceivable social structure. All human life and history, according to Leach, can be understood as an exploration of the infinite space of possibilities opened up by combining the different settings or values of a finite set of variables. This style of anthropological reasoning was not, in fact, original to Leach. Known in the trade as *structuralism*, it was introduced into the discipline by Claude Lévi-Strauss, arguably the most celebrated anthropologist of the second half of the twentieth century. Leach did much to bring this new way of thinking, arriving on English shores from France, to the attention of Anglophone scholarship. I remember listening in thrall to his lectures on the subject. To me, structuralism appealed as a kind of pure mathematics of social life.

Not long previously, in a study of scientific revolutions, philosopher Thomas Kuhn had coined the term 'paradigm' to denote the set of founding principles that, at any moment in the history of a discipline, constrain the questions it can ask and the means by which to resolve them.[2] In the previous chapter, I described how anthropology came of age within an evolutionary paradigm. Its leading question was: how do human beings, their artefacts and institutions *evolve*? We saw how this was overtaken, in social anthropology, by the paradigm of functionalism. It asked: how do institutions *work*? But with the paradigm of structuralism the question changed again. It became: how do the things people say and do *mean*? For structuralists, social life is enacted in communication, in the meaningful exchange of signs and symbols. Their key questions accordingly revolved around how signs and symbols can convey meaning, and how they relate to what they stand for. For answers, they turned to another discipline to which these questions had long been central, namely linguistics. All human languages have the remarkable property that while words are the smallest units that can carry meaning, they are comprised of still smaller units – technically known as phonemes but in alphabetical writing commonly rendered as letters – which, though without meaning in themselves, nevertheless enable speakers to distinguish one meaningful word from another. It is because of these distinctions, not in spite of them, that each word comes to mean what it does. Could these properties of linguistic communication be extended to other domains of social life?

In a course of lectures delivered at the University of Geneva between 1906 and 1911, the Swiss linguist Ferdinand de Saussure had argued that words generally mean what they do not because of any intrinsic connection between each word and each meaning, taken in isolation, but because of the way in which one system of contrasts, on the level of words, is mapped onto another, on the level of meanings.[3] To take a simple example, there is nothing inherently catty about the word 'cat', or doggy about the word 'dog', but by matching up the series of verbal contrasts between 'cat', 'dog' and all the other words for animal species with the series of taxonomic distinctions among the species themselves, a one-to-one correspondence is set up between words and kinds such that 'cat' and 'dog' line up, respectively, with feline and canine qualities. In a famous work on totemism – a term that describes the intimate bonds that in many societies are felt to exist between particular social groups and particular natural (often animal) kinds – Lévi-Strauss applied the same logic.[4] Here the 'words' are species in nature, their meanings are groups in society, and the totemic connection between a particular species and a certain group comes from mapping the differences between species onto the differences between groups. In this way, nature provides its own language, a set of concrete terms with which to represent the structure of society. If animals are often selected as totems, Lévi-Strauss concluded, it is because they are good not to eat but to think with.

But Lévi-Strauss went further, also applying to the social world a method developed by the Russian-American linguist Roman Jakobson for analysing the phonemes of any language as specific combinations of distinctive features, selected by that language from a limited repertoire of features available to all humans. The idea was that the same kind of distinctive feature analysis could work not only for the exchange of words, but also for the exchange of gifts and commodities in economic life and for the exchange of persons in forging relations of kinship and affinity. Following this logic, every society that has ever existed, or could ever exist, represents just one of countless combinatorial possibilities, all nevertheless underwritten by the architecture and generative potential of a universal human mind. Not for nothing has Lévi-Strauss been compared to an astronomer among social scientists, gazing at societies as if they were stars in the sky, each an object of distant contemplation. But in the infinitude of space and time wherein these stellar societies are arrayed, what has happened to the people? They appear to have vanished. If their existence is acknowledged at all, it is as accessories. They do not work through structures; structures work through them. Like the linguist who follows a conversation only for what it reveals about the deep structure of the language spoken by participants, but not for what they have to say and why, the structural anthropologist sees in the give and take of social life only the outward expression of unconscious structures of which the people themselves are wholly unaware.

While some anthropologists fancied themselves as astronomers, however, others went to the opposite extreme, resolving to re-enter social life at the atomic level. Their point of departure was individual human beings with values to pursue and limited resources for doing so, choosing at every turn to interact with one another only to secure the best strategic advantage. Suppose I have a sum of money and you have a watch. I really want your watch; you badly need the money. So we exchange – your watch for my money – and we both end up better off than before. For so-called *transactionalists*, all social interactions are of this kind, even if the values in exchange are immaterial, such as love or friendship. Theorists of this persuasion argued that forms of social organization are generated, and can therefore be explained, as the aggregate outcome of these myriad interactions, in each of which values of different kinds would be transacted. I myself was attracted by this approach, and by the time I graduated I was convinced that in it lay the future of social anthropology. Its leading advocate was the Norwegian anthropologist Fredrik Barth, then one of the towering figures in the discipline.[5] Like many of my contemporaries, I counted myself as an admirer, and as a beginning postgraduate student I resolved to spend some months in his department, at the University of Bergen, prior to commencing my doctoral fieldwork among Sami people in north-eastern Finland. Barth was a charismatic figure, whose inspirational presence matched the crystalline clarity of his prose. I was not disappointed.

But after sixteen months of fieldwork, more or less isolated from the academic environment, I returned to Bergen to find a department in turmoil. Barth had left for the United States, and transactionalism appeared on the verge of collapse. I discovered that while I had been away, a new circus had come to town, scattering everything in its path. In concert with budding political and intellectual movements in the Europe of the early 1970s, anthropology had rediscovered the philosophical work of Karl Marx, combining it with structuralism to form a hybrid strain going by the unwieldy name of 'structural Marxism'. Its promise was to bring the discipline back down to earth, from the rarefied mental space of combinatorial possibilities to the real world of human toil and historical transformation. There can, after all, be no social structures without people to enact them, and as Marx always insisted, there can be no people without the production of the necessities for life. Human beings have to produce their means of subsistence if life is to carry on, and this calls for some mode of practical engagement with the environment. The problem was that no environment, even the most extreme and unforgiving, actually tells people what to do. For human beings – if not perhaps for non-human animals – the intentions that drive the production of livelihood come from society. How, then, can the material conditions of human existence, and the constraints they impose, be reconciled with the relative autonomy of social structures in dictating the terms of environmental engagement? Structural Marxism offered a solution.

The problem itself was an old one, and went back to earlier attempts, principally in American anthropology, to establish a field of so-called 'cultural ecology', concerned specifically with the role of culture in human adaptation to the environment. It, too, was impaled on a dilemma. How can we hold, at one and the same time, that culture both drives what people do in their environment and furnishes the means by which they adapt to it? For theorists caught between cultural and environmental rationales for behaviour, there was no way forward but to opt for one or the other. Thus, some sought to show that customary beliefs and practices serve to maintain not just the social system of which they are a part but the entire ecosystem comprised by human relations with animals, plants and the land. Their assumption was that all such systems naturally incline towards equilibrium, since any that did not would have suffered long-term collapse. Others argued to the contrary, that beliefs and practices conform to a logic of their own, grounded in symbolic structures that owe nothing to environmental conditions. But neither option appeared viable. On the one hand, evidence for instability in human–environmental relations is everywhere; indeed it is the very engine of history. Why should human groups have ever transitioned from hunting and gathering to farming, or from extensive cultivation to intensive agriculture, were it not in response to population–resource imbalances? But on the other hand, are not these very transitions living proof that culture is not simply free to go its own way?

In 1974, as a newly appointed lecturer in social anthropology at Manchester University, I was given a course to teach called 'Environment and Technology', and these questions were at the heart of it. One hotly debated issue at the time, for example, concerned what was known as 'Wittfogel's hypothesis'. In a work entitled *Oriental Despotism*, published in 1957, the sinologist Karl Wittfogel had argued that the ancient empires of India and China, famed for their extreme oppression of the populace, had arisen in response to the demands of irrigation agriculture. The building and maintenance of irrigation works called for a massive input of labour that could only be mobilized and coordinated by a highly centralized and totalitarian regime. This argument was picked up by self-styled 'cultural materialists', who insisted that all forms of culture and social organization could be explained as necessary responses to techno-environmental conditions. Objectors, however, pointed out that irrigation agriculture was itself a means by which empires sought to consolidate and extend their power, since it supported ever-greater densities of population on the land. Thus the drivers were social and political, while the engineering of the environment lifted the bar on population density, allowing power to concentrate to previously unprecedented levels. A more recent example concerns the relation between the rise of industrial capitalism and the invention of the steam engine. Again, the engine was invented to meet the demands of capital, and not vice versa, yet it permitted a revolution in the scale of industrial production the like of which had never before been seen.

In the indigestible jargon of structural Marxism, this argument was expressed as the dialectic of dominance and determination. Dominant were the social structures and relations which governed the distribution of power and access to the means of production: land, resources and technology. Determinant were the ecosystemic dynamics of an environment modified to variable degrees by human intervention. The intensification of production, driven by dominant social relations, can eventually bring ecosystemic relations to breaking point, manifested, for example, as deforestation or desertification. Human history, in the Marxian narrative, is punctuated by crises of this kind, each of which can only be resolved by wholesale transformation in both social relations and techno-environmental conditions of production. With social evolution back on the agenda, now framed in Marxian rather than Darwinian terms, this was an approach around which social anthropologists and archaeologists, after decades of separation, could reunite. Both set about rewriting history, over the very long term, as a sequence of transformations running from the origins of agriculture to the industrial revolution. In fact, in the decades immediately preceding, archaeology had not remained immune from the upheavals in anthropological thought. Some – proponents of so-called 'processual archaeology' – had sought to interpret prehistoric artefact assemblages as evidence for human behavioural adaptation to environmental conditions; others – calling themselves 'post-processualists' – were determined to show how objects of material culture carried meanings constituted within wider fields of signification and figured in practice as vehicles of symbolic expression. Here, too, a Marxian approach to social evolution offered a potential resolution. But it was not to last.

The fall of structural Marxism was as sudden and astonishing as its rise. It came crashing down along with the Berlin Wall, in 1989, soon followed by the collapse of the Soviet Union and the declared end of the Cold War. Intellectuals – anthropologists among them – who had looked to Marx for inspiration went to ground or found other lights to follow. Scholarly tomes on pre-capitalist modes of production, once read by every student of anthropology, lay abandoned on library shelves, unopened and unloved. Indeed the shake-up of intellectual terrains was of such seismic proportions that many saw in it the end of an era that had encompassed the entire history of anthropology and related disciplines in the humanities, from their beginnings in the Enlightenment to the present. What we had witnessed, they declared, was nothing less than the demise of modernism. For when all is said and done, evolutionism, functionalism and structuralism were but variations on a modern theme. We had now crossed the threshold to a new era of postmodernism. All human life and history, it seemed, pivoted on the transition. For anthropology this meant a narrowing of temporal horizons from the grand sweep of social evolution to the contemporary pivot-point. At the same time it heralded a period of intense introspection, a questioning of traditional ways of working that had taken the sovereign authority of the western analyst for granted. For the postmodern world was also a postcolonial one, in which the intellectual pre-eminence of the West, and of those educated in its institutions, could no longer be assumed.

Closer to home, my own teaching had reached an impasse. Influenced by currents of thinking from both cultural ecology and structural Marxism, I had set out to show how every human being – at once a living organism bound with other organisms in what ecologists would call the 'web of life', and a person bound with other persons in a network of social relations – participates simultaneously in two systems, respectively ecological and social.[6] The problem, then, was to understand the interplay between the two systems: one dominant in furnishing productive activity with its intentions; the other determinant in setting limits to the pressure of production the environment could sustain. For example, in a society where men hunt and women gather, a man may intend to hunt in order to bring back meat to feed his family, but his harvesting is also subject to the ecological dynamics of predator–prey interaction. The latter might be understood by means of models drawn from the field of animal ecology, but understanding the former demands an approach from social anthropology. Neither could work on its own, I argued; we need rather to put them together. Yet I was increasingly troubled by this splitting of the human into two components, person and organism, partitioned respectively into the separate domains of society and nature. One day in 1988 it finally dawned on me that person and organism were not partners in human being but one and the same: that the organism-in-its-environment *is* a being-in-the-world. From that watershed moment, everything I had argued until then seemed irredeemably wrong.

To explain how I had reached this pass, we need to scroll back a couple of decades, to developments in the field until then known as physical anthropology. Here, too, there had been a pronounced shift, from a traditional concern with the evolution of human anatomy, as revealed in the fossil record, to concerns with behaviour and ecology. Comparing material from field studies of both human hunter-gatherers and non-human primates, behavioural ecologists were attempting to bring ancient humans to life by drawing inferences for the evolution of culture and social organization. Reflecting this shift from the fossil to the living, the sub-field had rechristened itself as 'biological' rather than 'physical'. At this time, too, many anthropologists had latched on to the idea of group selection. Already anticipated by Darwin in *The Descent of Man*, the idea was that natural selection operates at the group as well as the individual level. Working on individuals, selection would automatically favour the characteristics of the most fecund. But at the group level, there would be a selective bias towards mechanisms serving to limit reproduction and maintain numbers within sustainable limits. Groups possessing such mechanisms would achieve a lasting balance with their surroundings, while those without would eventually wipe themselves out through population growth and resource overload. This argument, as we have seen, also had its followers among social and cultural anthropologists. It purported to account for why social animals, such as humans, seemed so ready to put collective well-being before individual self-interest. In a word, it explained the phenomenon of altruism.

For behavioural ecologists, explaining altruism had become something of a holy grail, since it would at last provide a reason for why animals of so many species, the human included, live in societies. If you could explain altruism, they believed, you could explain society. But from the early 1970s, the weight of biological opinion came down against group selection and swung towards the other extreme. Selection really operates, many claimed, at neither the group nor the individual level, but at the level of the gene. As the chicken is for the egg, they argued, the individual organism is just a machine built by genes to secure their own propagation. Genes, however, are not unique to the individuals of a population but are shared to the degree that they are genealogically related. The more closely related you and I are, the more genes we have in common. In principle, then, a gene can further its own propagation by causing its carrier to behave in ways that disproportionately benefit relatives in which it is also represented, even at the carrier's own expense. Formulated as a rule by evolutionary biologist William Hamilton, if the gain in reproductive fitness to the beneficiaries, multiplied by the coefficient of genetic relatedness between beneficiaries and benefactor, exceeds the fitness cost to the benefactor, then kin-selection will tend to 'fix' the behaviour in question. Altruism, finally, had been shown to have a genetic explanation! And with that, a new discipline was born. Introduced with much fanfare by entomologist E.O. Wilson, it went by the name of 'sociobiology'.[7]

Social and cultural anthropologists reacted to these developments with dismay. Their objections were not so much to the theory itself as to the claim, enthusiastically put about by sociobiologists, that all social behaviour had been conclusively shown to have what was called a 'biological basis'. This raises the question, of course, of what a biological basis might be. Does 'biological' mean 'genetic'? And what does it mean to say of behaviour, anyway, that it is social? Does it imply cooperation among individuals that happen to be of the same species, whether ants in a colony, bees in a hive, elephants in a herd or humans in a community? That was Wilson's view. But against it, social anthropologist Meyer Fortes insisted that there could be no such thing as society or social relations without an instituted order, of a kind that depends on language and is unique to humans, and which defines persons as the occupants of positions vis-à-vis one another, as between parent and child in the family, teacher and pupil in the school, or doctor and patient in the surgery.[8] To extend the concept of society to the animal kingdom, Fortes argued, is to indulge in anthropomorphic metaphor. Sociobiologists were merely playing an old trick, of reading human forms of association into nature only to declare that society itself has a natural foundation. It is one thing to draw on our experience in the human community to describe the behaviour of 'social' insects, quite another to invert the metaphor and take the life of insects as a model for humanity.

A ferocious argument ensued, much of which centred on kinship – an old anthropological staple. Kinship is defined by genetic connection, declared those in one corner. No, said those in the other, it is a system of social categories; the probability of genetic connection between individuals placed in the categories is irrelevant. The behaviour of kin towards one another is governed by innate predisposition, insisted the first. No, countered the second, it is ruled by moral obligation. And anyway, they added, how would anyone know for sure who their genetic relatives are? That, retorted the first, is why everyone always crowds around a new baby to check on its resemblance to its various relatives. People are programmed to look out for tell-tale signs of genetic connection, to avoid being fooled into investing in individuals who don't carry their genes. Nonsense! cried the second; the commentary on resemblance is just part of the process whereby a persona – a name, and a place in the social order – is created for the new incumbent. And so it went on. Eventually, a truce was called. Neither side could have it completely their own way; instead, they settled on a compromise. Yes, human beings are innately predisposed to behave preferentially towards those with whom they have a genetic link, and yes, their behaviour is given meaning, and the persons to whom it is directed are categorized, in terms of an overarching order of relations. Each account gives us a partial description of kinship; to get the full picture we need to put the two together.

I call this compromise the thesis of complementarity. Person and organism, respectively social being and biological individual, are like two

Figure 4 Social relations are made in performance. Detail from
The Battle between Carnival and Lent (1559) by Pieter Bruegel
the Elder.
(Kunsthistorischen Wien)

complementary parts of the human which together
make the whole. What I realized, on that fateful
day in 1988, was that this bipartite conception of
the human, with one foot in nature and the other in
society, would have to go. For between genetic connection and social categorization, there is no room
for life. It falls through the cracks. In life, relations
are not given in advance but have continually to be
performed (see Figure 4). Relations of kinship, for
example, are performed in countless acts of care

and attention in which people are nourished, raised and educated. Yet the person nurtured within the matrix of kinship relations *is* an organism, growing in an environment that includes human and non-human others. Nurturance and growth are but two ways, respectively social and biological, of describing the same process of ontogenesis, of the continual generation of being – or in a word, of life. Any dispositions a person might have towards others, at any moment, will have arisen within this process. The love of parents for their children, for instance, arises from the prolonged intimacy of life in the home; it is not an effect of their probable genetic relatedness. But it is no less 'biological' for that. Humans, in short, are *biosocial beings*, not because they are products of genes and society, but because they continually produce themselves and one another as the living, breathing creatures they are. They are not two things but one.

The idea that human beings produce each other in body and mind, in the practical tasks of social life, now goes almost without saying. But it could only emerge thanks to one of the most profound shifts in the social anthropology of the past thirty years, from the predominantly structural thinking of previous decades to a way of thinking that focuses on relations not just as derivative of society, but as the very fabric of social life. Reality itself, we now assert, is relational through and through. This assertion, however, will not take us far unless we can specify more precisely what we mean by it. What is a social relation anyway? The question admits of three possible answers, only the last of which contains the germs of a truly relational ontology. The first answer is that every relation is a sequence of interactions, strung out over time. In an interaction, two parties meet and transact, while yet remaining by nature closed to one another. This answer underlies the transactionalist approach introduced earlier; as it does the sociobiological conception of society as an aggregate of interacting individuals of the same species. The second answer, by which social anthropologists sought to counter the sociobiological challenge, understands the relation quite differently, as existing not between individuals but between the positions they may occupy in an established institutional framework, such as between parent and child, teacher and pupil, doctor and patient. Precisely because each side in the sociobiology debate meant something different by the relation, they ended up talking past one another.

The third answer, however, is that relations are ways living beings have of going along together, and – as they do – of forging each other's existence.

Key, here, is the idea that in their unfolding, relations continually *give rise* to the beings they join. In anthropological jargon, beings-in-relation are 'mutually constituted'. To put it more simply, your relations with others get inside you and make you the being you are. And they get inside the others as well. So as you join with these others and, at the same time, differentiate yourself from them, this joining and differentiation proceed *from the inside*. Beings do not so much interact as *intra-act*; they are inside the action. The implications of relational thinking for what it means to be a person, or to exert agency in social affairs, remain key themes of current debate, much of it inspired by developments in feminist scholarship that have done so much to challenge the traditionally gendered polarization of male agency and female subjugation. Such thinking has, however, brought social anthropologists into renewed tension with their colleagues in mainstream biological anthropology, who remain largely faithful to the conventions of Darwinian evolutionary theory. The problem is that for the theory to work, every being has to be posited as a discrete individual, one of a population of such individuals, specified by an inheritance bestowed in advance of its life in the world, and relating to others along lines of external contact that leave its hereditary make-up unaffected. Biologists call this 'population thinking'. And it contradicts relational thinking at every turn.

Thus instead of the complementarity of two aspects of being, social and biological, we are now faced with a rupture between two ways of apprehending being itself – that is, two *ontologies* – respectively relational and populational. The sheer incompatibility of these ontologies is largely responsible for the current deadlock in negotiations between social and biological anthropology. To break the deadlock will require nothing less than a radically alternative biology – one that takes the living organism, as social anthropology now takes the person, to be fundamentally constituted in its relations with others. This kind of biology will require us to think of evolution not as change along lines of descent but as the unfolding of the entire relational matrix within which forms, both human and non-human, are generated and sustained. And it will require us to think of these forms as neither genetically nor culturally preconfigured but as ever-emergent outcomes of developmental or ontogenetic processes. This rethinking could amount to a revolution in the human sciences of our present century as great as if not greater than that wrought by the Darwinian paradigm for centuries past. The work that underpins it is going on now. In fields as diverse as molecular biology, epigenetics, immunology and neurophysiology, the biological sciences are in the throes of a paradigm shift towards a post-genomic world in which Darwinian logic no longer applies. This work is converging on a new synthesis, at once processual, developmental and relational. It has thrown the door wide open to contemporary anthropology. It is critical to the future of the discipline that we enter.

5

Anthropology for the Future

I hope to have convinced you by now that anthropology matters as never before. No other discipline is so pivotally positioned to bring to bear the weight of human experience, in every sphere of life, on the questions of how to forge a world fit for coming generations to inhabit. Yet in public debates on these questions anthropologists are for the most part conspicuous by their absence. Pundits of various disciplines strut the stage, offering their bite-sized assessments of our place in the world and their prognoses for the future. But where are anthropologists? Perhaps their absence has to do with the fact that they have no particular expertise they can call their own, nor any coherent body of knowledge to convey. The public reasonably looks to academic scholarship to provide answers to their questions. But the likely response of anthropologists is to take their questioners to task, to expose their implicit assumptions, to observe that other people – who do not make these assumptions – would pose the questions differently. There are no easy answers. Anthropology doesn't tell you what you want to know; it unsettles the foundations of what you thought you knew already. Students of the subject may end up knowing less than when they started, albeit wiser than before. This can be discomforting. And the commitment to take others seriously makes it unconscionable for anthropologists to pursue the strategy – followed by so many science writers – of tapping into the pre-existing appetites of their readers and furnishing the data and ideas, spiced with novelty, to satisfy them.

These appetites are not limited to a lay readership. They are shared, to a degree, by science itself. In one recent exchange, for example, evolutionary biologist (and titular anthropologist) David Sloan Wilson commends the work of anthropologists and others who – in his words – have 'compiled the vast storehouse of information about human cultures around the world and throughout history'.[1] That people are the creatures of their cultures, and that every culture can be laid up as a corpus of information for expert scrutiny, is assumed without question. The purpose of anthropological scholarship, in the view of Wilson and many more who think like him, is no more and no less than to harvest the material to be used to fill out a narrative that belongs to science. This narrative, of evolution through variation and selection, is for them unquestionable. You simply have to believe in it. Other people's beliefs may be grist to the mill of evolutionary explanation, but the belief in evolution is sacrosanct. Strictly speaking, this is not science but scientism. Science is a rich patchwork of knowledge which comes in an astonishing variety of different forms. Scientism is a doctrine, or system of beliefs, founded on the assertion that scientific knowledge takes but one form, and that this form has an unrivalled and universal claim to truth. Anthropology need have no problem with science. But against scientism it has reason to protest. To do so, however, anthropologists need to make their voices heard. They are presently hampered in this by three obstacles largely of their own making.

The first obstacle lies in anthropology's own self-presentation as the discipline that 'does' culture. Admittedly, not all anthropologists present their subject in this way, but many do. As a strategy, it is suicidal. It is understandable for every discipline to want to stake out its own territory, and if geographers have space, psychologists mind, biologists life and sociologists society, why shouldn't anthropologists stake their claim to culture? The problem is that in a capitalist regime in which the economy reigns supreme – in which human prosperity is supposed to depend upon the functioning of the market, in turn the foundation for society and the state – culture is like icing on the cake. Along with tourism, entertainment and sport, culture in such a regime turns other people's endeavours into commodities for our consumption and gratification. It is a luxury of affluence, and is therefore the first to go when austerity sets in. In so often presenting themselves as students of culture, anthropologists are virtually asking to be marginalized, especially when times are hard. Increasingly aware of this today, many anthropologists are dropping the dreaded 'culture' word, or doing their best to avoid it. Indeed one of the ironies of the present is that anthropology is seeking to divest itself of the concept of culture just as many other disciplines, long blind and deaf to human variation, are at last beginning to adopt it. But if anthropology abandons its stake in culture, what else can it do? This question bears on the issue of what 'discipline' means in academia, to which I shall turn shortly.

The second obstacle lies in anthropology's troubles with relativism. A statement entitled 'Why anthropology matters', prepared in 2015 by the Executive Committee of the European Association of Social Anthropologists (EASA), identifies cultural relativism as a key component of anthropological competence.[2] It is the view that the people of a culture judge their actions by their own lights, that these judgements have an internal logic or rationality of their own, and that none can be ranked better or worse on any absolute, culture-free scale of value. Another, less charitable way of putting this would be to say that for anthropology, anything goes, that human behaviour – even at its most grotesque and abhorrent – can always be excused on the grounds that it is 'part of the culture'. Anthropologists have been notoriously equivocal, for example, when it comes to notions of universal human rights, pointing out that they rest on ideas about individual entitlement, dignity and what it means to be human that have a particular history in the western world, and which often make little sense to the people among whom they have worked. Yet how, say anthropology's critics, can anyone take seriously the pronouncements of a discipline that professes to no moral compass of its own? A hard-line relativism would indeed be indefensible, for if everyone were so locked into their cultural worlds, no conversation would be possible, and anthropologists themselves would be out of a job. The alternative, however, is not to reassert universals of our own invention but to rejoin the conversation, in a spirit at once generous and critical.

Another component of anthropological competence identified by the EASA document is 'ethnography'. For the Committee, ethnography means participant observation. It sees them as the same thing. I already touched upon this confusion in Chapter 1, and I believe it to be the third obstacle that prevents anthropological voices from being properly heard. For ethnography bends participant observation to a purpose of its own, namely to distil the lives of others into an account, be it in writing or rendered by means of film or other graphic media. Good ethnography is sensitive, contextually nuanced, richly detailed and faithful to what it depicts. These are admirable qualities. But they do constrain the ethnographer, who must remain, if not hidden, then at least in the wings, allowing the people and their voices to take centre stage. It is their show, not the ethnographer's, even if they owe their write-up to him or her. Now if that were all there was to anthropology – if, as it seems to many, anthropology had contracted into ethnography – then those outside the discipline could be forgiven for concluding that anthropologists have nothing to

say for themselves, and that their role is only to provide the data on 'other cultures' the public expects
from them. They might even regard anthropology
as high-end journalism, distinguished by the excep-
tional richness of material that can only be gained
through deep and long-term immersion. Around the
world, indeed, ethnographers are currently embedded as reporters, sending back observations and
analysis from the field as if this, in itself, amounted
to a practice of anthropology.

But anthropology's purpose, in my view, is
entirely different. It is to draw on what we learn
from our education with other people to speculate
on what the conditions and possibilities of life
might be. As anthropologists, I believe, we should
cherish this freedom to speculate, to say what *we*
think, without pretending that our words are actually distillations of the views of the people among
whom we have studied. Had it not been for these
studies, of course, we could not say the things we
do. But it is not for us to speak on behalf of our
teachers. It is with *our* hearts and minds, not with
theirs, that we speak, and it is surely dishonest to
feign otherwise. Thanks to the wealth of human
experience we bring to the table, we anthropologists have hugely important things to say. We need
to be there to say them. If we are not, then others of

more intolerant or chauvinistic bent will be quick to fill the void. In what other discipline, after all, would practitioners forgo the privilege to speak out? If they can speak with their own voices, we can too. Moreover, once the aims of anthropology are decoupled from those of ethnography, all sorts of other ways are opened up to anthropology of joining the conversation, for example through practices of art, design, theatre, dance and music, not to mention architecture, museum studies and comparative history. Successful collaboration with practitioners in fields such as these depends precisely on the recognition that what we are doing is *not* ethnography.

Even discounting the obstacles set out above, anthropology still has a mountain to climb to correct the misunderstandings that plague its public profile. Popular stereotypes abound. One is of the intrepid fossil-hunter, determined to unearth the finds that will revolutionize the story of human origins – even to the extent of planting forgeries to deceive his colleagues. It took four decades for Piltdown Man, 'discovered' in 1912 in a Sussex gravel pit, to be revealed as a hoax. The forger's identity remains unknown, but we have already met a prime suspect in Chapter 3: none other than Sir Arthur Keith, who in 1938 unveiled a memorial to the find and its 'discoverer', one Charles Dawson.

Pictures of the creature christened *Eoanthropus
dawsoni* – strikingly hirsute, spear in one hand and
stone axe in the other – long graced the pages of
popular magazines. How convenient that the miss-
ing link between ape and man lay in the heart of
England! For those raised on the modern myth of
origin – that at some mighty moment in the past
our brilliant ancestors broke the bonds of nature
to commence their inexorable rise to civilization –
finding the first humans remains a topic of enduring
fascination. The currently favoured out-of-Africa
hypothesis has a race of superior beings dispersing
from its African cradle to colonize the world. It
is a hypothesis that strikingly resembles the story
of colonial conquest by White Europeans favoured
by Darwin and his contemporaries. The story may
have been turned upside down, but the structure is
the same: one dominant race, equipped with superior intelligence, supersedes the rest.

At the other extreme is the stereotype of the
anthropologist embarked on a fool's errand, to
discover cultures untainted by contact with civilization. This was brilliantly parodied in a 1984
cartoon from *The Far Side*, by Gary Larson. Three
native gentlemen are at home. Catching sight of
approaching visitors, one lets out a warning cry:
'Anthropologists! Anthropologists!' The other two

scurry to hide their equipment, including television, video recorder, phone and electric light. The anthropologists of the cartoon are looking for authentic otherness, but their quest is doomed, for the people are already cheerfully enjoying the benefits of civilization. In this as in many films and novels, the anthropologist is lampooned as a figure of fun, duped by the natives into falling for a charade. In a well-known spoof, dating from 1956, the American anthropologist Horace Miner attempted to turn the tables on his own kind. His paper, entitled 'Body ritual among the Nacirema', described a backward tribe of North America with a still little-known culture, whose rituals included daily insertion into the mouth of a bundle of hog-hairs daubed with magical powders, and annual visits to holy mouth-men.[3] The Nacirema also had healing temples, known as *latipso*, where gruesome rites were carried out on sickly natives, many of whom would never return. It is hard to understand, Miner concluded, how such a magic-ridden people had existed for so long. For in the myth of authenticity, pristine cultures are always on the verge of disappearing, as their traditional ways, caught in a repetitive present, are overtaken by the linear march of progress.

These stereotypes of the anthropologist as either villain or fool, and the myths of origin and authenticity on which they are founded, are hard to dislodge. In the media, fossil skulls vie for attention with depictions of tribal peoples dressed in traditional costume, or no costume at all, inviting viewers to compare the contemporary exotic with the ancestral past. Meanwhile, popularizers with no anthropological knowledge or training, but with some experience of living with remote people, are keen to present themselves as anthropologists, and to peddle widespread fictions about the human condition as if they were the fruits of scientific research. Their books have been best-sellers. If professional anthropologists presume to object, the press is only too happy to present their complaints as sour grapes or academic infighting. No wonder many anthropologists feel the odds are stacked against them, much as they often are for the people among whom they work. To change the odds in our favour, I believe we need to do three things. The first is to re-establish anthropology as a single discipline, rather than a congeries of separate sub-disciplines. The second is to achieve a new settlement between anthropologists of sociocultural and biophysical disposition, whose current antagonism threatens to blow the discipline apart, and this means confronting the twin spectres of culture and race. The third is to show how a future anthropology that is speculative and experimental, as well as descriptive and analytic, could have the potential to transform lives. In the remainder of this chapter I shall address each of these ambitions in turn.

Some years ago, I had the opportunity to develop a new programme in anthropology here at the University of Aberdeen. As it began to take shape, we had to decide what to call it. Should it be known as 'social anthropology' or plain 'anthropology'? By training, I and my colleagues were social anthropologists. We nevertheless decided to go for 'anthropology'. One reason, banal but significant, was that anthropology begins with an A. In these days of drop-down menus, where everything is in alphabetical order, what better way to signal that anthropology matters than by putting it at the top of the list! There was, however, another reason of greater import. It was the conviction that the programme we aimed to develop, and to present to our students, should be a discipline in its own right and not a specialized subdivision of something greater, and that its concern should accordingly be with human life in the round rather than with any particular facet of it. This did, however, raise the question of what it means to say, of a subject like anthropology, that it is a 'discipline' at all. If, as I have argued, it is a way of studying *with* people

117

rather than making studies *of* them, how can it lay claim to any intellectual territory of its own? Insofar as it refuses any such claim, anthropology could truly be said to be an *anti-discipline*. For it will have no truck with the kind of intellectual colonialism that divides the world of knowledge into separate parcels for each discipline to rule.

But there's another way of imagining the discipline that better reflects on anthropological practice. This is to think of it as a conversation, and of its practitioners as a community of scholars. What we learned about communities in general, in Chapter 2, would then apply to disciplines specifically. In them, people are joined by their differences rather than united in the defence of common territory. It is not therefore for anthropology to stake an exclusive claim to culture or anything else. The landscape of scholarship, like that of social life itself, is continuous. In it, anthropologists follow their noses, sniffing out promising sources and lines of inquiry. They are like hunters on the trail. To hunt, you have to dream the animal; get under its skin to perceive as it does; know it from the inside out. And you have to attend closely to what is going on around and about, and to what it has to tell you. So too with anthropology: it is about following one's dreams, getting under the skin of the world, know-

118

ing from the inside and learning from observation. Anthropology, then, lays a medley of trails, as hunters do, through the landscape of human experience. The recent proliferation of anthropologies – medical, visual, environmental, cognitive, and so on – of which some were listed in Chapter 3, does not consequently portend the fragmentation of the discipline. For each affords a certain means of finding one's way about in the medley. And it is the threading of every trail through a continuous landscape that binds them into one conversation.

This was the spirit in which we resolved in our programme to address human being in the round. The glue that holds anthropology together, we insisted, is the unity of experience. Anthropologists often express this unity with the concept of *holism*. By this they mean that the task of anthropology is to focus on the entwinement of aspects of life that might otherwise be apportioned between different disciplines for separate study. Thus economists might study the market, political scientists the state and theologians the church, but anthropologists set out to show how market, state and church interpenetrate in people's experience. Likewise, we refuse to accept that human life can be sliced into layers, of body, mind and society, or that its study can be divided between biologists, psychologists and sociologists. Anthropology's subject is humanity unsliced. A classical statement of this position came from Marcel Mauss, a founding figure of French ethnology, in an essay on body techniques dating from 1934. To focus only on biological and socio-logical aspects of human being is not enough, Mauss argued, since it leaves out what he called the 'psy-chological mediator'. Mind necessarily intervenes between body and society. We need, he declared, a 'triple viewpoint, that of the "total man"'.[4] This idea of totality holds its dangers, however. For it posits a complete human whose very existence is encompassed and contained. Yet without loose ends, life cannot continue. It must always escape. Holism and totalization, then, are not the same, for by the former we mean life's infinitude rather than the finality of joined-up being.

Anthropology, in short, is a discipline that works by entering into the life process and going along with it. This, perhaps, will help answer a question often posed by students new to the subject. How does anthropology differ from sociology? Some might answer that it does not. Recall that for Radcliffe-Brown, social anthropology was itself a branch of sociology, distinguished by its attention to societies once called simple, small-scale and traditional. This distinction no longer applies today. It is as usual, in our time, for anthropologists to be working at home as abroad, and in major metropolitan centres as in rural peripheries. Sociologists, for their part, have added ethnography to their armoury of research methods, and mix qualitative with quantitative data in their analyses. In many university departments and degree programmes, sociology and anthropology are frictionlessly combined. Yet many anthropologists, including myself, still sense a deep difference between the two disciplines. Though hard to pin down, I believe it has to do with the enduring legacy of that great mid-twentieth-century experiment known as 'social science'. It was an experiment launched on the promise that the facts of society could be recorded and analysed with the same objectivity and authority as those of nature, yielding up to rigorous scientific understanding. This promise was summed up in one word, 'positivism'. The subsequent career of social science has been dogged by interminable arguments between the advocates of positivism and its opponents. And it was in the heat of these arguments that the discipline of sociology was forged in its modern form.

In all this, however, anthropology remained a bystander. Already divided down the middle between its scientific and humanistic wings, respectively biophysical and sociocultural, it had little to invest in a project that sought to bring science to the study of social phenomena. Radcliffe-Brown's proposal to establish social anthropology as what he called a 'natural science of society' never really took off. Rather than aligning with positivist science, anthropologists of a social and cultural inclination turned increasingly for inspiration to other approaches in the humanities, in history, philosophy, comparative religion and studies of language and literature. Nor could sociocultural anthropologists ever quite reconcile themselves to the way in which ethnography – *their* word, by which they actually meant participant observation – had been appropriated by sociologists and other social scientists to cover almost any technique of questioning or interview capable of yielding qualitative data for analysis, even if it involved no sustained participation or observational engagement at all. Today, the project of social science has largely burnt itself out, paralysed by its lingering commitment to a positivism long since abandoned even by the 'harder' sciences, and by irresolvable disputes concerning the very possibility of objective inquiry into the forms of human life. It survives as little more than a coalition of disciplines, from economics and management studies to education and social psychology, assembled more for administrative convenience than on any grounds of intellectual coherence. Even when formally classified as a social science, anthropology has only a tenuous foothold there. I believe the future of the discipline lies elsewhere, in the contemporary convergence of science with art.

We cannot turn to this convergence, however, before confronting two inner demons, which remain to be exorcized if anthropology is to have a future at all. They are the demons of race and culture. Anthropologists are sometimes accused of worrying incessantly over the meanings of words, when they should be engaging with facts on the ground. But for anyone who thinks that words don't matter, the examples of 'race' and 'culture' should give pause. 'The race concept', as the American anthropologist Eric Wolf once put it, 'has presided over homicide and genocide.'[5] Wolf was writing in the early 1990s, when the war in the Balkans was at its peak, and entire communities were being wiped out in operations of 'ethnic cleansing'. Here culture, not race, supplied the massacre with its motive, but for those affected the consequences were no less devastating. What principles, then, combine in the concepts of race and culture to make them such potentially explosive weapons of mass destruction? There are two, *essentialism* and *inheritance*, each harmless on its own, but in combination lethal. Essentialism is the doctrine, already touched upon in Chapter 2, that a group is categorically defined by its members' having certain attributes in common. Inheritance is the principle whereby these attributes are bestowed on recipients in each generation, independently and in advance of their life in the world. The mechanism of inheritance may be genetic or imitative, the attributes innate or acquired. The logic is the same for both. And wedded to essentialist thinking, this logic remains deeply embedded within the anthropological constitution.

Anthropologists have tried two ways to detoxify their discipline of racial thinking. The first, on which I have already remarked, was to narrow the classification of extant humans from the species to the sub-species level. Yet far from renouncing the concept of race, to say that all humans are of one sub-species affirms it. It is to claim not just that race exists, but that in deep prehistory there were indeed distinct races of humankind. The story is told of how ancestral creatures of our own kind overran the continent of Europe at the expense of its indigenous Neanderthal population, humans of a different sub-species. The ill-fated Neanderthals are thought to have become extinct some forty thousand years ago, but for many millennia previously they had lived alongside humans of our sort, and even interbred with them. Had we been alive in the Palaeolithic, would it then have been acceptable to speak of the races of man? It is still widely believed that our ancestors won out thanks to their possession of attributes, common to all modern humans but lacking in their competitors, that have been lodged in our genes ever since. Nor is this blend of essentialism and inheritance shaken by the second way in which anthropologists have attempted to erase the scourge of racial thinking, namely by substituting heritage for heredity. Humans, they claim, are divided not by race but by culture. Yet the reasoning that leads anthropologists to assert the existence of discrete cultures would, if reapplied to genetically inherited variation, lead straight back to the existence of race.

In short, in their eagerness to repudiate the science of race, anthropologists have contrived to reproduce the very principles that give rise to it. To appreciate how this came about, we need to return to the settlement which originally set physical and cultural anthropology on their separate trajectories. Originally established by Kroeber, in his 1917 paper on 'The superorganic', it asserted the complete independence of biological and cultural variation, allowing the study of each to proceed more or less independently of the other. As we saw in Chapter 3, the settlement came into effect sooner on the cultural than on the biological side, allowing an explicitly racial science to flourish in physical anthropology right up until the end of the Second World War. But anthropologists of the post-war era, haunted by the racism that had so disfigured their discipline in the interwar years, could no longer bring themselves to allow that cultural differences could themselves be biological. The idea was literally unthinkable. This consensus was reiterated in a 'Statement on race', issued in 1996 by the American Association of Physical Anthropologists (AAPA).[6] The statement opens with the assertion that 'there is no necessary concordance between biological characteristics and culturally defined groups', and concludes that 'it is not justifiable to attribute cultural characteristics to the influence of genetic inheritance'. These words repay attention, for in them lies the germ of the very thinking the statement claims to demolish. It is the attribution of what at the start are called 'biological characteristics' to what in the end is called 'genetic inheritance'.

The real source of the problem lies not – as Kroeber thought and as is reiterated by the AAPA – in the confusion of cultural with biological characteristics. It lies in the attribution of the latter to inherited genes. And this attribution remains at the heart of evolutionary approaches which purport to factor out human variation into inherited components, respectively 'biological' and 'cultural', and to regard every human being as a hybrid compound of the two. Theories of biocultural evolution, based on the idea of dual or 'twin-track' inheritance – one working through genetic replication, the other through its learning-based analogue – continue to command popular support. But these theories, as we saw in Chapter 2, are inherently circular, positing the outcomes of ontogenetic development as their cause. It is the logic of inheritance that pretends to close the circle, by installing the properties of the developing organism prior to the processes that give rise to them. Inheritance serves here as a logical short-cut, bypassing the path of development. This path, however, points the way to a new settlement, which rests on the premise that biological properties *are themselves culturally differentiated*. What was inconceivable for the anthropology of the twentieth century, that cultural and biological variations are concordant, is emerging as foundational for the anthropology of the twenty-first. It is borne out in studies of neuroplasticity that demonstrate the malleability to experience of the developing brain, in studies of how movement trains the body and perception the senses, and even in studies of anatomy which reveal the effects of nutrition and activity on skeletal growth.

By liberating biological variation from the shackles of genetic inheritance, and cultural difference from the yoke of heritage, we can finally lay the demons of race and culture to rest. Humanity is indivisible into discrete races for precisely the same reason that it is indivisible into discrete cultures. That reason lies in history. Human beings, as agents of history, have ever been the producers of their lives. This history, moreover, is part of a life process that is going on throughout the organic world. Call the process evolution if you will, but this is not what most students of evolutionary anthropology mean by the term. Looking back, it is a tragedy of anthropology that the conditions of exchange between the discipline's sociocultural and bio-physical wings were set by a paradigm of evolution couched in narrowly Darwinian terms. In its current, neo-Darwinian incarnation, the paradigm is both uncompromising in its focus on the calculus of inheritance and intolerant of critique. For anthropology, it represents a cul-de-sac. Theorists who would treat real people as no more than cartoonish animations of their inherited characteristics have, of their own accord, excluded themselves from the conversation. They can play no part in any future anthropology that professes to take others seriously. One of the great upcoming challenges of anthropology, I believe, will be to shift the grounds of evolutionary science. Like a super-tanker on the high seas, it will be slow to turn. But turn it eventually will. When it does, anthropology will at last rediscover its unity in the richness and indivisibility of human experience.

Will this anthropology, then, be science or art? Earlier, I compared the anthropologist to a hunter: a dreamer, a follower of life's ways who learns from observation and gets under the skin of things to know them from the inside. It is arguably the role of art to do the same: to reawaken our senses, allowing knowledge to grow from the inside of being in the unfolding of life. As that most anthropological of artists, Paul Klee, declared in his 'Creative credo' of 1920: 'Art does not reproduce the visible but makes visible.'[7] Klee's maxim applies with equal force to anthropology. It is not for art or for anthropology to hold a mirror to the world. It is rather to enter into the relations and processes that give rise to worldly things so as to bring them into the field of our awareness. And like art, anthropology need not be wedded only to describing and analysing things as they are. It, too, can be experimental, and given to speculation. The anthropologist's field is not of

129

course a laboratory, and is no place for experiments in the scientific sense of artfully setting up a scenario in order to test a preconceived hypothesis. But as in every moment of our quotidian lives, we can experiment by intervening in things, and by following where our interventions lead. This is to ask questions of others, and of the world, and to wait upon their answers. It is what happens in any conversation. And like all conversations, it changes the lives of everyone involved.

But the anthropological conversation, thus conceived as an art of inquiry, need not be opposed to science. It rather points towards a different way of *doing* science – more modest, humane and sustainable than much of what passes for science today. It is a way that joins with the world rather than arrogating exclusive powers to explicate it. Anthropology aspires neither to reduce all things to data nor to convert these data into products, or what research policymakers call 'outputs'. True, like scholars of other disciplines, we publish books and articles, amass a literature comprised of the worthy contributions of predecessors, and demand of students that they read it. But that is not what ultimately matters. Anthropology's real contribution lies not in its literature but in its capacity to transform lives. This is why the idea of 'applied anthropology' has so little traction in the discipline. It is not that we want to keep our knowledge to ourselves, pure and untainted by use, but because there can be no knowledge that does not itself grow from our practical engagement with others. For what drives anthropologists, in the final resort, is not the demand for knowledge but an ethic of care. We don't care for others by treating them as objects of investigation, by assigning them to categories and contexts or by explaining them away. We care by bringing them into presence, so that they can converse with us, and we can learn from them. That's the way to build a world with room for everyone. We can only build it together.

Notes

Chapter 1 On Taking Others Seriously

1 Marx's observation comes from his essay of 1852, *The Eighteenth Brumaire of Louis Bonaparte*: 'Men make their own history', he wrote, 'but they do not make it as they please; they do not make it under self-selected circumstances, but under circumstances existing already, given and transmitted from the past.'

2 Arif E. Jinha, 'Article 50 million: an estimate of the number of scholarly articles in existence', *Learned Publishing* 23 (2010): 258–63.

3 A. Irving Hallowell, 'Ojibwa ontology, behavior and world view', in *Culture in History: Essays in Honor of Paul Radin*, ed. Stanley Diamond (New York: Columbia University Press, 1960), pp. 19–52. The quotation is from p. 24.

4 Émile Durkheim, *The Elementary Forms of the Religious Life*, trans. Joseph Ward Swain, 2nd edition (London: Allen & Unwin, 1976).

Chapter 2 Similarity and Difference

1 Giorgio Agamben, *The Open: Man and Animal*, trans. Kevin Attell (Stanford, CA: Stanford University Press, 2004), p. 27.

2 Richard Dawkins, *The Selfish Gene* (Oxford: Oxford University Press, 1976); Susan Blackmore, *The Meme Machine* (Oxford: Oxford University Press, 1999).

3 Henrietta Moore, *A Passion for Difference: Essays in Anthropology and Gender* (Bloomington: Indiana University Press, 1994).

4 Donald Brown, *Human Universals* (New York: McGraw-Hill, 1991).

5 Steven Pinker, *The Language Instinct* (New York: William Morrow, 1994).

6 Geertz's essay, 'The impact of culture on the concept of man', was first published in 1966. See Clifford Geertz, *The Interpretation of Cultures* (London: Fontana, 1973), pp. 33–54. The quotation is from p. 45.

7 John Tooby and Leda Cosmides, 'The psychological foundations of culture', in *The Adapted Mind: Evolutionary Psychology and the Generation of Culture*, eds Jerome H. Barkow, Leda Cosmides and John Tooby (New York: Oxford University Press, 1992), pp. 19–136. The quotation is from p. 33.

8 Edmund Leach, *A Runaway World?* (London: Oxford University Press, 1967), p. 34.

9 Bruno Latour, *We Have Never Been Modern*, trans. Catherine Porter (Cambridge, MA: Harvard University Press, 1991).

Chapter 3 A Discipline Divided

1 Thomas Henry Huxley, *Man's Place in Nature and Other Essays* (London: Macmillan, 1894), p. 152.
2 Robert W. Reid, *Inaugural Lecture: The Development of Anthropology in the University of Aberdeen* (Aberdeen: Aberdeen University Press, 1934), p. 18.
3 Arthur Keith, *The Place of Prejudice in Modern Civilization* (London: Williams & Norgate, 1931), p. 49.
4 Alfred Reginald Radcliffe-Brown, *Structure and Function in Primitive Society* (London: Cohen & West, 1952), p. 2.
5 Marshall Sahlins, *Stone Age Economics* (London: Tavistock, 1972), p. 81. Sahlins does not name his source.
6 Alfred L. Kroeber, 'The superorganic' (1917), in his *The Nature of Culture* (Chicago: University of Chicago Press, 1952), pp. 22–51.

Chapter 4 Rethinking the Social

1 Edmund Leach, *Rethinking Anthropology* (London: Athlone Press, 1961), pp. 2–3.
2 Thomas Kuhn, *The Structure of Scientific Revolutions* (Chicago: University of Chicago Press, 1962).
3 Ferdinand de Saussure, *Course in General Linguistics*, eds Charles Bally and Albert Sechehaye, trans. Wade Baskin (New York: Philosophical Library, 1959).
4 Claude Lévi-Strauss, *Totemism*, trans. Rodney Needham (London: Merlin Press, 1964).

5 Fredrik Barth, *Models of Social Organization* (Royal Anthropological Institute Occasional Paper 23) (London: Royal Anthropological Institute, 1966).

6 Tim Ingold, *The Appropriation of Nature: Essays on Human Ecology and Social Relations* (Manchester: Manchester University Press, 1986).

7 Edward O. Wilson, *Sociobiology: The New Synthesis* (Cambridge, MA: Harvard University Press, 1975).

8 Meyer Fortes, *Rules and the Emergence of Society* (Royal Anthropological Institute Occasional Paper 39) (London: Royal Anthropological Institute, 1983).

Chapter 5 Anthropology for the Future

1 David Sloan Wilson, 'The One Culture: four new books indicate that the barrier between science and the humanities is at last breaking down', *Social Evolution Forum, The Evolution Institute*, 2016, available at *https://evolution-institute.org/focus-article/the-one-culture/?source=sef*.

2 European Association of Social Anthropologists, 'Why anthropology matters', Prague, 15 October 2015, available at *https://www.easaonline.org/downloads/publications/policy/EASA%20policy%20paper_EN.pdf*.

3 Horace Miner, 'Body ritual among the Nacirema', *American Anthropologist* 58 (1956): 503–7.

4 Marcel Mauss, 'Body techniques' [1934], in *Sociology and Psychology: Essays by Marcel Mauss*, trans. Ben Brewster, Part IV (London: Routledge and Kegan Paul, 1979), pp. 97–123. The quotation is from p. 101.

5 Eric Wolf, 'Perilous ideas: race, culture, people', *Current Anthropology* 35 (1994): 1–12.
6 American Association of Physical Anthropologists, 'Statement on biological aspects of race', *American Journal of Physical Anthropology* 101 (1996): 569–70.
7 Paul Klee, *Notebooks, Volume I: The Thinking Eye*, ed. Jürg Spiller, trans. Ralph Mannheim (London: Lund Humphries, 1961), p. 76.

Further Reading

Introductions to social
and cultural anthropology

Joy Hendry. *An Introduction to Social Anthropology: Sharing Our Worlds.* New York: Palgrave, 2016.

John Monaghan and Peter Just. *Social and Cultural Anthropology: A Very Short Introduction.* Oxford: Oxford University Press, 2000.

Thomas Hylland Eriksen. *Small Places, Large Issues: An Introduction to Social and Cultural Anthropology.* London: Pluto Press, 1995.

Michael Carrithers. *Why Humans Have Cultures: Explaining Anthropology and Social Diversity.* Oxford: Oxford University Press, 1992.

General works worth looking at

Tim Ingold, ed. *Key Debates in Anthropology.* London: Routledge, 1996.

Further Reading

Adam Kuper. *Anthropology and Anthropologists: The Modern British School* (3rd edition). London: Routledge, 1996.

Clifford Geertz. *The Interpretation of Cultures*. London: Fontana, 1973.

Works of reference

Nigel Rapport and Joanna Overing. *Social and Cultural Anthropology: The Key Concepts*. London: Routledge, 2000.

Alan Barnard and Jonathan Spencer. *Encyclopedia of Social and Cultural Anthropology*. London: Routledge, 1996.

Tim Ingold, ed. *Companion Encyclopedia of Anthropology: Humanity, Culture and Social Life*. London: Routledge, 1994.

Index

Agamben, Giorgio 29
ageing 39
agency and gender 103
agriculture
    irrigation 90
    origins and intensification
        of 89, 92
altruism 96–7
American Association of
        Physical Anthropologists
        (AAPA) 126
animism 23
Anthropocene 5
anthropology
    applied 130–1
    and art 113,129
    comparative 25, 80–1
    and the concept of culture
        108–9
    defined 4
    for the future 2, 116–17
    history of 2, 15, 56–7
    as hunting 118–19, 129

and journalism 112
for one world 27
versus philosophy 2–3
public profile of 57, 106–7,
        113, 116
purpose of 8–9, 14, 25,
        107–8, 112
'three-field' 66–7, 69–70,
        78
varieties of 54–6
'we' of 51
see also archaeology;
        biological anthropology;
        cultural anthropology;
        ethnography; linguistic
        anthropology; physical
        anthropology; social
        anthropology
Anthropos 29
archaeology 66, 70–1, 73,
        78
    processual versus post-
        processual 92

Index

art
    and anthropology 113, 129
    human capacity for 40
    of inquiry 130
    and science 129–30
attention 9, 11, 22
    in kinship 101

Barth, Fredrik 87
behaviour
    causes of 30–1
    cultural and environmental
        rationales for 89
    and ecology 95–6
    sociobiological explanation
        of 97–9
Berens, William 17–24
biodiversity 28
biological anthropology 95
    versus social or cultural
        anthropology 54–5, 74,
        78, 103–4, 121, 128
    see also physical
        anthropology
biological characteristics
    versus cultural
        characteristics 30, 74,
        125–8
    see also genes; heritage;
        inheritance
biology 74
    evolutionary 78
    relational 104
    see also sociobiology
Boas, Franz 76
Brown, Donald 32–3

Burnett James (Lord
    Monboddo) 59–60

care 9
    and kinship 100
    ethic of 131
categorization 45
civilization
    contact with 114–15
    ills of 35
    rise of 57, 60, 63, 65, 114
climate change 5
colonialism 25, 77, 114
    intellectual 93, 118
communication 83-4
community 47–50
    of scholars 118
complementarity, thesis of
    99–100, 104
conversation
    anthropological 110–11,
        130
    and community 47
    discipline as 118–19
    world as 25
Cosmides, Leda 44
cultural anthropology 75–8,
    125
    see also social
        anthropology
cultural characteristics versus
    biological characteristics
    30, 74, 125–8
    see also genes; heritage;
        inheritance
cultural ecology 88–9, 94

Index

cultural materialism 90
culture
  capacity for 41–2
  concept of 16, 108–9
  and diversity 26
  and nature 27–8, 33, 37,
    44
  as a question 30
  and race 73–6, 123–5, 128
cycling 39

Darwin, Charles
  on the descent of man
    62–3, 95
  on the natives of Tierra del
    Fuego 61
  not a Darwinist 65
Darwinism, social 65
data 12, 130
  quantitative versus
    qualitative 12, 121
Dawkins, Richard 31
discipline, academic 117–18
distinctive feature analysis 85
dominance
  versus determination 91,
    94
dreaming 21
Durkheim, Émile 19

ecology 28, 94
  behavioural 95–6
  cultural 88–9, 94
education 10, 14
Eibl-Eibesfeldt, Irenäus 13
embodiment 38–9

Enlightenment 57–8, 77, 93
epistemology versus ontology
    17
essentialism 27, 123–4
ethnicity 48, 123
ethnography 13, 55, 111,
    121–2
  versus anthropology 14,
    111–13
  and participant
    observation 13–14, 111,
    122
ethnology 75
eugenics 65
European Association of
    Social Anthropologists
    (EASA) 110–11
evolution
  as an anthropological
    paradigm 83, 93
  as a life process 128–9
  social 71–2, 91–3
  study of 55, 66, 103–4
experience 21
  and imagination 8, 10, 17,
    21–2
  unity of 119

feminism 103
Ferguson, Adam 58
field versus laboratory 11–12,
    129–30
fieldwork, anthropological 11
Fitzroy, Robert 60–1, 65
Fortes, Meyer 98
functionalism 72–3, 83, 93

Index

Geertz, Clifford 43
gender and agency 103
genes 31
  and environment 36
  and inheritance 126
  and kinship 98–9
  and selection 96–7
gift 11
group selection 95–6

Hallowell, A. Irving 17–20,
  24
Hamilton, William 97
heritage
  defence of 48, 50
  versus heredity 74, 76,
    125, 128
  see also inheritance
history 4, 6, 39–40, 91–3,
  128
Hobbes, Thomas 57
holism 119
Homo (genus, in the order of
  Primates) 58–9
Homo sapiens 2, 29, 69
human rights 69, 110
humanity, idea of 29–30, 54
humans 1–2
  versus animals 1, 29, 43,
    62–3
  versus apes 60
  as biosocial beings 101
  classification of 58–60
hunter-gatherers 33–5, 40,
  94–5
Huxley, Thomas Henry 63–4

identity 46–8
imagination and experience
  8, 10, 17, 21–2
improvisation 1
information 6–8
inheritance 123–7
  of acquired characteristics
    73–4
  dual 127
  and population thinking
    103
  see also heritage
instinct 35–6
  for language 37
intelligence
  evolution of 62–3
  and head-size 67
interaction 102
  versus intra-action 103

Jakobson, Roman 85

Keith, Arthur 68, 113
kinship 98–101
Klee, Paul 129
knowledge 6–7
  production of 8
  versus wisdom 9–10
Kroeber, Alfred 74–6,
  125–6
Kuhn, Thomas 82

laboratory versus field 11–12,
  129–30
Lamarck, Jean-Baptiste 74
language, acquisition of 37

Index

Latour, Bruno 49
Leach, Edmund 46, 81–2
Lévi-Strauss, Claude 82, 84–5
life
  as circulation of materials and energy 23
  convergence and divergence in 45
  as conversation 25
  ways of 1–2
Linnaeus, Carolus 58–60
linguistic anthropology 78
linguistics 83–5
Locke, John 58

Marx, Karl 6, 87–8, 92
Marxism, structural 88, 91–2, 94
material conditions 88
Mauss, Marcel 120
memes 31
methods 10–11
mind
  and body 76, 119–20
  human 60
  and matter 28
  progress of 62
  universal 85
modernism, and postmodernism 93
modernity
  values of 49
museum, anthropological 67
museum studies 55, 113

Nacirema, body rituals of 115
natural selection 33, 63, 95–6, 108
nature
  and culture 27–8, 33, 37, 44
  human 40–1, 44
  versus humanity 50, 54, 69
  meaning of 27-8
  versus nurture 36
  as a question 30, 44
  versus society 94, 98, 100, 121
  state of 57
Neanderthals 124

objectivity 8–9, 11, 21, 121
Ojibwa people (north-central Canada) 17–20, 24, 32
ontogenesis 36, 101, 104, 127
  and embodiment 38-9
ontology
  versus epistemology 17
  relational versus populational 104
  turn to 24
organism versus person 94–5, 99–101

paradigm
  Darwinian 104–5, 128
  defined 82-3

143

Index

participant observation 11–12
and ethnography 13–14, 111, 122
performance, social relations made in 100
person
versus organism 94–5, 99–101
relational 103–4
in society 98
philosophy 2–3
physical anthropology 66, 70–1, 73–4, 78, 95, 126
and biological anthropology 95
Piltdown Man 113–14
population, global 4
population thinking versus relational thinking 103–4
positivism 121–2
presence 8–9, 12, 22, 131
primates, non-human 58, 95
production
industrial 91
of livelihood 88
pressure of 91, 94
progress, myth of 41, 115
psychic unity of mankind, doctrine of 64
psychology 28, 120
evolutionary 44, 55

race
and culture 73–4, 76, 116, 123–5, 128
science of 125–6
racial thinking 67–8
Radcliffe-Brown, Alfred Reginald 70, 79–81, 120, 122
rapport 13
reason 40
Reid, Robert 67
relational thinking 103–4
relations
meaning of 102
performance of 100–1
relativism 109–10
religion 19, 23
ritual 20
Romanticism 76–7
Rousseau, Jean-Jacques 58
Royal Anthropological Institute 66

sacred versus profane 19
Sahlins, Marshall 73
Saussure, Ferdinand de 84
science 7, 40, 52–3
and art 129–30
versus humanities 53–4
and scientism 108
snakes, fear of 32–4
social anthropology 70–4, 77–8, 83, 87, 120
and animal ecology 94
versus 'anthropology' 117
comparative 79–80

Index

versus cultural
  anthropology 75, 77
as a natural science of
  society 122
from structural to
  relational thinking in
  101
social life, 2, 100–2
  biological basis of 97
  fluidity of 81
social science 78, 121–3
society
  concept of 98
  existence of 80
  explaining 96
  versus nature 94, 98, 100,
    121
  'primitive' 79
sociobiology 97–8, 102
sociology 19, 122
  versus anthropology 120–1
  social anthropology a
    branch of 70, 75, 79,
    120
speech 21–2, 37
  and toolmaking 33–4
stones, animacy of 19–23
structuralism 82–6, 93
symbols, meanings of 83

technology
  capacity for 40
  and environment 90
Tooby, John 44
toolmaking 33–4
totemism 84–5
transactionalism 86–7,
  102
truth 21

universals 32–3, 110–11
  genetic traits as 31
  and particulars 28, 38,
    42–3, 50

walking 1, 38, 40
  and place 47
  and talking 43–4
westerners, absence of
  49–50
wheel, invention of 39
Wilson, David Sloan 107
Wilson, E.O. 97–8
wisdom 2
  versus knowledge
    9–10
Wittfogel's hypothesis 90
Wolf, Eric 123
writing, by hand 39